Springfield & Clark County

AN ILLUS-TRATED HISTORY

Springfield & Clark County

AN ILLUS-TRATED HISTORY

BY WILLIAM A. KINNISON
PICTURE RESEARCH BY F. KENNETH DICKERSON
PARTNERS IN PROGRESS BY JON L. JOYCE

PRODUCED IN COOPERATION WITH THE
CLARK COUNTY HISTORICAL SOCIETY AND
WITTENBERG UNIVERSITY

WINDSOR PUBLICATIONS, INC.
NORTHRIDGE, CALIFORNIA

Page 2
Following World War II there was a boom economy for Springfield and Clark County. Traffic was heavy at the Big Four Station, pictured on a cold winter morning circa 1950. This view looks east along Washington Street. To the left is the Arcade Hotel. Courtesy, Springfield Newspapers, Inc.

IN MEMORY OF R. CARLTON BAUER, LONGTIME MEMBER OF THE BOARD OF DIRECTORS OF THE CLARK COUNTY HISTORICAL SOCIETY

Windsor Publications, Inc.—History Book Division
Publisher: John M. Phillips
Editorial Director: Teri Davis Greenberg
Design Director: Alexander D'Anca

Staff for *Springfield & Clark County*
Senior Editor: Michelle Hudun
Editorial Development: Annette Igra, Sarah Tringali
Director, Corporate Biographies: Karen Story
Assistant Director, Corporate Biographies: Phyllis Gray
Editor, Corporate Biographies: Judith Hunter
Editorial Assistants: Kathy M. Brown, Patricia Cobb, Gail Koffman, Lonnie Pham, Pat Pittman
Designer: Ellen Ifrah
Layout Artist: Walt Shelly

Library of Congress Cataloging in Publication Data
Kinnison, William A.   1932-
   Springfield & Clark County.

   Bibliography: p. 148
   Includes index.
   1. Springfield (Ohio)—History. 2. Springfield (Ohio)—Description. 3. Springfield (Ohio)—Industries. 4. Clark County (Ohio)—History. 5. Clark County (Ohio)—Description and travel. 6. Clark County (Ohio)—Industries. I. Dickerson, F. Kenneth. II. Title. III. Title: Springfield and Clark County.
F499.S7K56 1985   977.1'49   85-6553
ISBN 0-89781-146-1

Contents

Preface

From its earliest years Springfield has been engaged in rugged competition with other towns in Southwestern Ohio: Dayton, Columbus, Xenia, and Urbana, among others. Once that competition brought communities together. Competing for people, canals, the National Road, railroads, colleges, business, and industry gave everyone in town a reason to feel a part of things. The level of competition became so high and extended, over such a long period of time, that cooperation among the cities in Southwestern Ohio was more to be hoped for than an actual reality.

Another effect of continuing competition, however, was an estrangement of sorts between city and county, employer and employee, north side and south side. Most parties, it seemed, had been so busy with their own problems and their own opportunities that their lives evolved without much attention to their interrelationships, being together in a single geographic area. Now that modern mass media, mass marketing, electronic communications, and rapid transportation have freed individuals from total dependence on the communities in which they live, the unity and cohesion have been further dissipated while the rivalries and the competition have become global. At each stage along the way, as this process has evolved, those who found their lives rooted in Springfield and Clark County strove to put together the best community they could under the circumstances.

The history of the area is both the story of the development of competition and estrangement and also of the efforts of men and women to put the community together anew in each succeeding generation. It is hoped that this history will help today's citizens fulfill their responsibilities for life together by better understanding how we arrived at where we are today, and how past generations went about solving their problems of community.

There are cities in the world that are hundreds, and even thousands, of years old. By comparison Springfield and Clark County is a youthful community indeed. The city of Springfield will be a mere 200 years old in 1999, and settlement in what later became Clark County can be said to have started two centuries ago by 1995.

The coming of these bicentennials should be a signal to all of us to find bases for the renewal of our community life in this very livable place we call Springfield and Clark County. It is to that end that the effort to produce this history is directed. The best is yet to come.

Acknowledgments

No one person writes the history of a community. Springfield and Clark County has had a long tradition of historians, chroniclers, and recorders to whom any subsequent writer is indebted. Perhaps the earliest is R.G. Woodward, city librarian, who first chronicled area developments in 1856. Second was Oscar T. Martin who wrote a history of the city in 1881, and Alden P. Steele who wrote a general history of Clark County during the same year. F.M. McAdams, James Arbogast, Madison Over, Dr. H.H. Young, Daniel Baker, and Perry Stewart wrote histories of all the townships. These efforts were put together in what is commonly referred to as *Beer's History,* named after the publisher.

In 1908 William A. Rockel published his history, entitled *20th Century History of Springfield and Clark County, Ohio, and Representative Citizens.* Then in 1922 Benjamin F. Prince, the "Grand Old Man" of Wittenberg and a resident of Springfield since he came as a student in 1862, wrote *A Standard History of Springfield and Clark County.* The most recent history of Springfield and Clark County was produced by writers of the Works Project Administration (WPA) in 1941.

A special word of appreciation must be expressed for the continuing encouragement given by the Clark County Commission to the Clark County Historical Society. For several decades the county commissioners have provided support for the society, and its current commissioners—Merle G. Kearns, Louis I. Kerrigan, and J. Newton Oliver—have continued that support. Their help has been particularly beneficial in enabling the membership to fund an annual publication that has encouraged a continuing exploration of specific topics and issues in area history. A large number of those publications are listed in the bibliography, and this writer owes a particular debt of gratitude to those officers and editors, including: Willard D. Allbeck, George H. Berkhofer, David R. Collins, Guy G. Miller, Mary McGregor Miller, Dorothy Brain Mills, Orton G. Rust, Mary A. Skardon, and J. Martin West.

Floyd Barmann, director-curator of the Clark County Historical Society, F. Kenneth Dickerson of Wittenberg University, and Jon Joyce of Clark Technical College have provided very special assistance in a variety of ways,

as has my secretary, Barbara Johnson, whose editorial skills greatly improved this narrative. The editors of Windsor Publications, Inc., Michelle Hudun, Annette Igra, and Sarah Tringali, were able to see the story as a whole, as well as in its parts, and bring it to a consistency of style which was admirable indeed.

The Board of Directors of the Clark County Historical Society were enthusiastic in their endorsement and sponsorship of this project, and the author is particularly indebted to them. They deserve the thanks of all of us for their guardianship of the history and tradition of Springfield and Clark County. Members include: Mr. Robert Bare, Mr. John Bartley, Mr. Paul Ballentine, Dr. Paul Buchanan, Mrs. Linda Davis, Mrs. Alice Kinnard, Mr. W. Emerson Reck, Mr. Mitchell Reedy, Mr. Jerry E. Rinker, Mrs. Reed Robertson, Mrs. Udean Smith, Mr. William Hugh Smith, Mrs. Charles Stahl, Mr. John Tehan, and Mr. Lynn Zechman.

Equally deserving of our appreciation are the members of the Advisory Committee, which was appointed by the Clark County Historical Society to assist in putting this project together. The members were: Dr. John Buscher, Mr. James Foreman, Mrs. Merle Kearns, Mr. William Lambacher, Mrs. G. Samuel Lambert, Dr. Lloyd Monnin, and Mr. Michael Trempe. Society board members Robert Bare and George Raup were also members of the committee. To them we express the thanks of everyone involved.

A most important word of thanks needs to be expressed to Mary M. Miller, who agreed to read the entire manuscript for errors of omission and errors of commission. Her broad knowledge of the community's history and her own writing skills were invaluable.

I express thanks also to Wittenberg University for the sabbatical leave which enabled me to work on this project and for its help in so many other ways.

None of the above, however, share any blame for errors remaining or matters omitted because of space limitations. All, and especially my wife Lenore and my children William, Linda, and Amy, have been very supportive of this effort and share major responsibility for whatever success attends it.

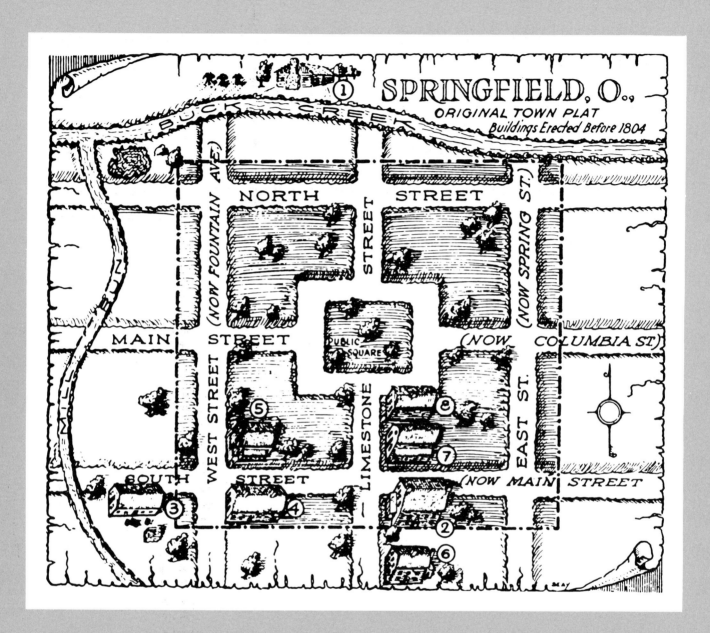

1

A Rich and Empty Land

This was a rich and empty land before the white man came. Indian hunters roamed the forests seeking buffalo, elk, bear, and deer. There were no permanent settlements, but it had not always been so. The area was too bountiful to be unoccupied.

Eons ago the land lay at the bottom of a sea. When earthquakes thrust up the land, vast water supplies were captured in a great underground river, and the fields abounded in fresh water and mineral springs. There were limestone rock formations of such quality that area builders later named the rock Springfield stone. Along with the stone came supplies of lime, clay, sand, and gravel— and some of the most fertile soil in America. During the first glacial period the valley became the haunt of the mastodon and other gigantic animals, and, along with fossils of minute sea creatures, their remains can still be found.

In time abundant forests grew to cover the rich soil. The woods were so thick that Indians claimed a bird could fly from Kentucky to Lake Erie without landing on the ground. Beech, maple, oak, hickory, poplar, walnut, ash, elm, sycamore, and buckeye trees were plentiful, along with fruit trees, wild berries, and grapes. An early frontiersman said his horse was stained red in a day's ride through the countryside, so thick were the berries.

The woods were stocked with game of all varieties— ducks, geese, wild turkeys, partridges, and other edible game birds, as well as robins, blue jays, cardinals, and bobolinks, bees, and butterflies. The streams contained fish aplenty, frogs, and crawling things. Amid beautiful evergreens, dense shrubbery, grapes, and berries grew hazel and plum thickets, roses, the yellow flames of witch hazel, closed gentians, and cardinal flowers—flowers of every kind. The streams and swamps were marked by waving cattails, marsh grass, and sparkling pools.

Wandering hunters entered the area in 11,000 B.C. Then in 3000 B.C. a group called the Archaic People hunted, fished, and gathered food in the valleys and hills. They were more sedentary than the earlier wanderers but were not farmers. Two millenia later the Glacial Kame culture left evidence of its rudimentary civilization.

The earliest culture apparent to white settlers was that of the Mound Builders, who occupied the area from about 700 B.C. to about A.D. 600, during what are called the Early, Middle, and Late Woodland periods. The Adena, Hopewell, and Fort Ancient people (using the names given to them today) were characteristic of the three periods. These ancient ancestors of the American Indian left many remains in the valleys of the Little and Great Miami rivers. Mounds, forts, and earthwork enclosures were found by pioneers, along with village sites, artifacts, tools, and weapons.

Why these people vanished and their relationship to the Indians remain mysteries. The last of the Fort Ancient people vanished before 1600, at about the time the Erie Culture, or Indian Cat Nation, moved into Ohio. Within fifty years the Erie themselves were destroyed or routed

by the Iroquois Six Nations. Those who had occupied the area disappeared, and newcomers were run off or killed by Indians from the east. Thereafter, the Ohio country was again uninhabited.

Into the emptiness that was Ohio came French and English hunters and trappers, together with parties of the many different Indian tribes that roamed the area. Increasing numbers of French and English frontiersmen tarried to collect pelts and hides they could barter at the more permanent trading posts that developed. Indians who had a sense of the free use of the land became increasingly alarmed by these folks who stayed in rudimentary cabins.

The Ohio country was a connecting link between the Great Lakes to the north and the Ohio River to the south. The streams feeding each, which stretched toward one another like so many fingers in the middle of the Ohio territory, made the land a highway. Ohio was also the ground between the English to the east and the lands they coveted further west. The earliest highways were buffalo trails and streams. The French and English learned to use them from the Indians. One such highway, running northwest from the Ohio River, passed between the fresh water and the mineral springs in the area now called Springfield. Hunters, trappers, and, later, more permanent settlers followed these natural trails.

In the early eighteenth century the Miami Indians moved from Wisconsin into the more hospitable climate of Ohio. At the same time the Shawnee migrated from Georgia. There is evidence that the Fort Ancient people may have been the ancestors of the nomadic Shawnee, and the Shawnee trek to Ohio was, as they claimed, a return to their ancestral lands. By 1750 the Shawnee were established in the Scioto River Valley. As they spread their settlement over Southern and Central Ohio, they were determined not to move or to be pushed out again.

Pictured is an enlarged woodcut view of Piqua, taken from Howe's History of Ohio, *published in 1848. The log house on the hill to the upper left of the center is presumed to be the one Jonathan Donnel erected from 1795 to 1796 on a portion of the Indian fort site. To the far right are the few remaining structures of the town of New Boston. The Lower Valley Pike winds through the center of the picture. Courtesy, Clark County Historical Society (CCHS)*

They offered stiff resistance to white settlers. Other tribes also moved in. The Wyandots came from Canada and the Delawares came from the eastern seaboard. Ottawas and Mingos also appeared. The Mad River Valley, with its herb gardens and mineral springs, became a favorite hunting ground and a medicinal retreat.

Yet white men were also attracted. Virginia's colonial charter included extensive western holdings, and in 1748 entrepreneurs created the Ohio Land Company. Christopher Gist was sent to explore Ohio and report back. During Gist's journeys in the spring of 1751, he saw the flooded stream which roared through the valley nearly a mile wide, and he christened it the Mad River. The area Gist explored later came to be known as the Mad River Valley.

The French were interested in Ohio as well. They established an outpost as early as 1720 at the Shawnee village of Piqua, west of the site where Springfield was later established, in order to trade with the Indians.

By 1755 the British and French were at war in Europe and in America, in what Americans called the French and Indian War. The Indians were inclined to side with the French because they did not settle permanently the way the British did. The French merely passed through, temporarily using the area, while the English planned to re-

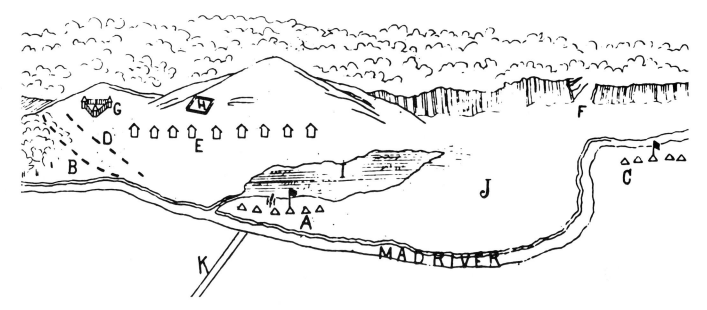

This woodcut depicts Thomas McGrew's hypothetical plan of the 1780 Battle of Piqua. From 1875 to 1880 McGrew composed several manuscripts on Piqua that sparked local interest and resulted in the Centennial of the Battle in 1880. The plan, originally drawn in 1875, was published in the June 14, 1880, edition of The Springfield Republic. Later scholarship proved this concept incorrect. CCHS

main, demanding others recognize their claim and stay out. General Edward Braddock's defeat in 1755 at Fort Duquesne in Pennsylvania sent tribes flocking to the side of the French who, it appeared, would be victorious. Being on the winning side, the Indians felt they would gain more or, perhaps, lose less.

By 1763, however, the British had won. Looking for breathing room in determining colonial Indian policy in the newly won territory, the British government established the Proclamation Line of 1763. It prohibited further western migration by white settlers. The action became one of a growing number of disagreements between the Americans and the mother country. Eastern colonists wanted buffers between themselves and the Indians. Those headed west wanted the opportunity to inhabit the Ohio country. Westerners and westward-moving colonists violated the Proclamation Line.

Indians continued to attack white settlements in Kentucky and western Virginia, as well as parties of hunters in Ohio. In 1774 Lord Dunmore, the governor of Virginia, raised an army of Virginia and Kentucky settlers and moved northward to attack the Indians in Ohio. His objective was to pacify the Ohio River Valley and stop Indian raids on white settlers. Lord Dunmore's War, as the frontiersmen called it, blended into the American Revolution, which began two years later. The frontier was aflame as the British mobilized the Indians against the settlements.

As the Revolution continued, an important battle was fought in the Springfield area: the Battle of Piqua. This battle was the result of a coordinated British-Indian invasion of Kentucky, led by Colonel Henry Bird, in which two white settlements were destroyed. It was part of a general offensive aimed at destroying the town of Louisville.

Lack of supplies, heavy rains, and the unruly actions of the Indians caused Bird to retreat.

In August 1780 General George Rogers Clark organized an army of 1,000 Kentuckians to move north against the retreating British and their Indian allies. He landed near where Cincinnati now stands and moved immediately against the Shawnee town of Chillicothe, twelve miles south of Springfield at Old Town. He arrived in time to see the burning huts of the Indians, who had abandoned the area and fled to their capital at Piqua.

Two days later Clark's troops attacked Piqua, which extended three miles along the north shore of Mad River. It was protected by Indian forts, built under British supervision, and was surrounded by acres of corn and great fields of vegetables. The battle, according to Clark, "opened with a savage fierceness" along a mile-wide front. The Indians were forced out of their positions on the hills and driven into their forts, from which they were routed by Clark's cannon. A twelve-year-old Indian named Tecumseh watched the battle from the fork of a tree. Later he escaped with the main body of Indians.

At nightfall, after six hours of fighting, the remaining Indians were routed. They retreated northward along the base of the cliffs bordering the river. The Aberfelda Ravine offered them the opportunity to escape. Indian losses were heavy, nearly four times those of the Kentuckians.

Clark's retaliation was so successful that there were no further Shawnee attacks against Kentucky settlements for two years. Joint Indian and British action became defensive and sporadic.

When Clark's troops returned home to Kentucky, many were unable to forget the beautiful Ohio country. They longed to possess the lands over which they had just fought. Even after Cornwallis surrendered, however, Indian warfare continued in the Ohio country, preventing white settlement. Yet although the land could not be settled, it was being provided for politically. The Ohio country was ceded to the American Confederacy in 1783 by the Treaty of Paris, and the various states that held title to western lands ceded them to the New Republic.

Virginia asked that the United States award tracts to Virginians who had served in the Revolution. This request led to the creation of the Virginia Military District, which included lands later incorporated in Clark County. The provision greatly influenced settlement. Connecticut retained a Western Reserve—a northeastern corner of Ohio—with which to meet its Revolutionary obligations. These reserves and other early land grants brought settlers from a number of regions of the New Republic to Ohio. For example John Cleves Symmes of New Jersey was allowed to purchase one million acres between the Great and Little Miami rivers, including most of what later became Clark County. He was unable to pay for all the land, however, and returned most of it to the government in 1794. Nevertheless he attracted large numbers of New Jersey settlers to the area.

Congress enacted the Ordinance of 1787, which set forth the basic principles for the organization and governance of the Northwest Territories. It provided for the admission of new states, granted self-government to the people even before statehood, provided for public education, set property requirements for voters and for election to office, and prohibited slavery.

By 1790 the fertile soil, wooded hills, abundant game, and sparkling, fish-filled waters that Clark's men had seen prompted some of them to return. Among the veterans of the Battle of Piqua was John Paul, who became the area's first settler. He erected his cabin on Honey Creek and with his wife and three children began clearing the area and planting crops. Within weeks Indians attacked, killing all except one son and one daughter.

Settlement was a dangerous matter. That same year the Indians, under Little Turtle, had defeated General Josiah Harmar at Fort Wayne. In 1791 they defeated General St. Clair's troops at Fort Recovery. General George Washington then picked General "Mad Anthony" Wayne to pacify the frontier. Wayne, a distinguished military man, was considered reckless in battle, hence his nickname. In 1794 Wayne won a decisive victory at Fallen

Timbers in Northwestern Ohio. The Treaty of Greenville, signed in 1795, ceded Southwestern Ohio.

Following the signing of the treaty, settlements became more frequent. In 1795 David Lowry and Jonathan Donnel, both from Pennsylvania, built homes west of Mad River. Lowry came to Ohio in 1794 and worked in Cincinnati, packing provisions for General Wayne's army. He then joined a surveying company, working for Donnel, and spent several days surveying the Mad River area. Lowry and Donnel were so impressed by the potential of the valley that they decided to buy the lands. The owner, Patten Shorts, a Cincinnati land speculator, agreed to sell the portion they wanted in return for their further services.

The following year two other men, Kreb and Brown, settled and raised the area's first crop of corn. Lowry hunted and fished to supply them with food while they cultivated the crop in which he later shared. According to Lowry he also built the first flatboat "that ever navigated

Skilled, fearless, and gallant Revolutionary War General "Mad Anthony" Wayne, pictured circa 1783, was appointed general-in-chief by President George Washington in 1792 and launched an expedition against the Indians of the Northwest the next year. After a campaign of sixteen months Wayne's army met 2,000 Shawnees led by Blue Jacket at Fallen Timbers (above present Maumee, Ohio) in August of 1794. Wayne's victory was decisive and the resulting Treaty of Greenville signed in August 1795 by more than ninety Indian representatives ended Indian warfare in Ohio. CCHS

the Big Miami from Dayton down." He ran errands for the surveyor and for the farmers, and in 1800 took venison hams, pickled pork, and bacon to Cincinnati and New Orleans. Later he drove hogs from Dayton to Cincinnati and there prepared them for market. He developed a barrel-making enterprise with William Ross in Dayton.

In 1798 James Galloway came from Pennsylvania by way of Kentucky. He later moved further south into what is now Greene County. In 1799 John Humphreys came with Simon Kenton and six other families from Kentucky and founded the first settlements that were to become Springfield. The party included James Demint, Philip Jarbo, William Ward, John Richards, William Moore, and one other. They settled where Buck Creek flowed into Mad River. In the fall they erected a fort, fourteen cabins, and a blockhouse for protection. James Demint, formerly a teamster for a Kentucky surveying company, moved up Buck Creek and built his cabin on its north side, over-

Simon Kenton became a frontier legend. In 1780 he was a guide for George Rogers Clark at the Battle of Piqua, and then for Colonel Benjamin Logan in sorties against Shawnees in Logan County in 1786. In 1799 Kenton, by then a man of affairs, settled in Springfield. With companions he built a fort at the fork of the Mad River and Lagonda (now Buck) Creek, presently the site of the Ohio Edison Plant. CCHS

looking the land to the south. Two years later he laid out a town there. He called the town Springfield, at the suggestion of his wife and Mrs. Simon Kenton. Kenton himself settled with his wife and ten slaves a few miles north of Buck Creek. The three settlements—Humphreys', Demint's, and Kenton's—marked the dimensions of the town to be.

For Kenton, it was not his first trip to the area. In 1778 some friends and he had stolen seven horses from the Shawnee near Old Town. Kenton was captured and taken to the Indian village of Chillicothe (Old Town) where he was sentenced to death. Before execution, however, Kenton was forced to brave the gauntlet, running between a double row of Indians, each armed with a club. If a prisoner ran the gauntlet and was able to reach the council tent, his ordeal was over. If he failed, he might be beaten to death or made to run it again. Kenton succeeded yet because of his great size, strength, and bushy red hair he was taken on tour of the Indian villages. He survived gauntlet after gauntlet and was finally sold to the British in Detroit where he recuperated. He later escaped and returned to Kentucky.

Having lost his land claims in Kentucky, Kenton decided to move to the Ohio country. In 1802 Kenton built a gristmill, carding machine, and sawmill on the narrow gorge of the creek. The area developed into the village of Lagonda. Kenton staked out squatter's rights on this area as he had done with land in Kentucky. Friends of the pioneer induced Congress to donate a tract of thirty acres covering his improvements. In 1814 Kenton sold the property to William Ward, one of the original pioneers who traveled with Kenton from Kentucky.

The next group to come to the area was headed by Griffith Foos and also from Kentucky. The migrants traveled up the Scioto River to Franklinton, a village west of the site where Columbus is now located. Considering the area swampy and unhealthy, Foos and a small party set out to find a better place. In 1801 they came upon the spot where James Demint planned to lay out the town of Springfield. They were in search of the beautiful Mad River Valley that hunters had told them about. They stopped to rest at a large spring of excellent water near the present corner of Main and Spring streets. After several days they came upon Demint's cabin, where they rested and enjoyed Mrs. Demint's hospitality.

Demint offered Foos several lots at very low rates if he would bring his entire party there to settle. Another visitor at the Demints' was John Dougherty, a surveyor. With Foos' commitment to settle, Demint hired Dougherty to lay out the town. The original plat was for a town of eighty-two lots that ran from the creek to half a block south of today's Columbia Street and from Fountain to Spring Street.

Griffith Foos and his traveling party returned to the Scioto for their families. On the return trip they made the first wagon track into the town from the east, and it took them four-and-a-half days to make the forty-mile trip. They cut their way through the forest and the underbrush and forded streams. In crossing the Big Darby they transported their goods on horses and drew the wagons across with ropes while some swam alongside to prevent an upset.

Griffith Foos is clearly entitled to equal honors with James Demint as founder of the city. Contemporaries saw him as a man of better habits and greater industry. If Demint was the typical frontiersman, Foos was the typical go-getter who brought energy and industry to frontier settlements. By June of 1801 Foos had erected the first building on the south side of the creek, a log house that served as a tavern for travelers and settlers alike. Across the creek James Demint established a still and a gristmill in 1803. Meanwhile Dougherty, the surveyor, decided to stay in the area. He became very popular among the settlers, who often elected him their representative in political matters. In 1804 he was named the town's first postmaster.

Mrs. Walter Smallwood, an organizer of the Methodist Society in Springfield, described the village as it appeared in 1804. There were eleven houses, all built of logs. In addition, there was John Reed's cooper shop; Charles Stowe's dry goods and grocery store; a store "in which a couple of Frenchmen kept a few dry goods for sale"; and two taverns, one operated by Griffith Foos and another by Archibald Lowry, David Lowry's brother. Three houses had stone chimneys, which were considered an ornament and evidence of prosperity. In the same year, Archibald Lowry built Springfield's first "good house." It was frame instead of log.

Although there was no church building, Methodist preachers on the Miami circuit came to the village every three or four weeks. The services were held in Foos' tavern. Occasionally, a traveling Baptist preacher appeared. The visits of preachers, like the coming of visitors in general, increased when a road was completed between Springfield and Dayton by David Lowry and others in 1803. The entire population turned out to finish the last few miles in a single day, then returned to Foos' tavern to celebrate. In 1805 a road was completed between Springfield and Franklinton, and the citizens celebrated again.

In 1806 Nathaniel Pinkered opened a school in a log cabin on the corner of Main and Market streets. That fall a Methodist Episcopal Church was formally organized with a dozen or so members. Services moved from Foos' tavern to Pinkered's schoolhouse. The circuit riders continued to come periodically, but in between visits the parishioners looked after their own spiritual welfare.

The village was beginning to reap benefits from its water supply. There were no streams of consequence nearer than Chillicothe, sixty miles southeast, so the villagers started building mills of various kinds. In 1807 Robert Rennix built a flour mill and a gristmill on Buck Creek near Mill Run, and the citizens celebrated these additions to their comfort and convenience. Two years later John Lingle and Jacob Cook built a powder mill to meet another frontier necessity.

The desire for a better supply of gunpowder was growing. Fear of Indian uprisings increased. In the Treaty of Greenville of 1795 the Indians had supposedly ceded Southern Ohio to the United States goverment. Yet Indians continued to appear in parties of two or three, in small bands, and occasionally in larger groups. Like the white men they encountered, some were friendly and some were not. They came to hunt in their favorite areas and to use the convenient trails. Many did not understand the concept of land ownership, and they resented the white man's habit of marking off lands as personal and private property. Some denied the right of those who signed the Treaty of Greenville to give the lands away. The Shawnee, in particular, felt that their rights in the area had not been properly represented.

During the summer of 1806, anxieties were heightened by rumors that Tecumseh had returned and was forming a new Indian nation. Citizens rushed to take cover in a two-story log house at High and Limestone streets and kept watch until the alarm subsided. In the fall of 1807 a white man was killed by Indians near Urbana. The incident together with Tecumseh's efforts aroused fears once again.

Tecumseh, the twelve-year-old who had watched the Battle of Piqua from the fork of a tree, had grown up to become an ambitious leader of his people. He envisioned a plan that would unite all the different tribes remaining in the Ohio country. The Shawnee were no longer strong enough to withstand the white man alone, but Tecumseh preached strength in unity. When he asked for command of the remnants of the Shawnee nation to show other tribes that the Shawnee could lead the general uprising, he met strong opposition from other Shawnee chiefs. This disharmony was hidden from the settlers, however, and their fears remained.

General William Henry Harrison, a popular leader in Southwest Ohio and a frequent visitor to Springfield, warned that Tecumseh was a born leader, an indefatigable worker, and a brilliant and moving orator. "Were it not for the vicinity of the United States," he added, "Tecumseh would be the founder of an empire that would rival Mexico or Peru."

Fears became so great that some left Springfield to return to former homes. Foos' house was again converted to

William Henry Harrison, pictured circa 1812, was aide-de-camp to General "Mad Anthony" Wayne in the Battle of Fallen Timbers on August 20, 1794. In May of 1800, President John Adams appointed him governor of the Indiana Territory, where Harrison recognized Tecumseh's genius for leadership and organization. A brigadier general in the War of 1812, Harrison commanded troops who defeated the British at the Battle of the Thames, in which Tecumseh died. Harrison resigned his commission in 1814 and was appointed to negotiate a second Treaty of Greenville. Elected president and inaugurated March 4, 1841, he died one month later on April 4th and was the first U.S. president to die in office. CCHS

a fort. Yet Tecumseh did not want the murder near Urbana to force him into premature conflict. The Shawnee, he said, were innocent, and he agreed to a council to discuss the problem.

At this time, according to legend, Tecumseh was courting Rebecca Galloway, daughter of James and Rebecca Galloway, who settled in Greene County in 1799. His own feelings toward whites were ambivalent. When Tecumseh asked Rebecca to marry him, she said she would if he assumed the ways of the white man. Tecumseh said that he could not accept those conditions without losing respect and leadership among the Shawnee.

In late summer of 1807, a council was held in Richard Hunt's sugar-maple grove near Main and Spring streets, across from Foos' tavern. Those present at the council included Hunt, Jonah Baldwin, John Humphreys, Simon Kenton, Walter Smallwood, John Dougherty, and Griffith Foos. The Indians were represented by five or six chiefs, the leader of whom was Tecumseh. Sixty or so braves and

as many white settlers were present.

As the council began, Tecumseh refused to allow the Indians to be disarmed, and when Hunt offered him a clay pipe to smoke, he indignantly refused it and threw it into the field.

It became clear that Tecumseh and his party were not responsible for the slaying. Tecumseh made what observers described as a very animated and fluent speech in which he denied all hostile intentions. The council ended with a guarantee of peace and security for the inhabitants of the village of Springfield.

Following the council, the Indians remained for three days. There was a friendly spirit, and the Indians and the whites participated in games and athletic contests of running, throwing, jumping, and wrestling. Area residents marveled at Tecumseh's strength and athletic prowess. Henry Howe, an early Ohio historian, described him as one of remarkable strength and power, equal to his high intellect and moral character.

After the council there was no more trouble. Tecumseh and the Shawnees were not finished with their conflict with the United States, but the chief's pledge to the Springfielders was never broken, perhaps as his final gift to Rebecca Galloway.

By 1810 Tecumseh and his brother, The Prophet, attempted to put their coalition of Indians to effective use. General William Henry Harrison kept an eye on the Shawnee chief. "You see him today on the Wabash," he said, "and in a short time hear of him on the shores of Lake Erie or Lake Michigan or on the banks of the Mississippi; and wherever he goes, he makes an impression favorable to his purpose."

Harrison marched on the Indians while Tecumseh was away. The Prophet sought to achieve a victory in Tecumseh's absence and played into Harrison's hands. Harrison defeated the Shawnee and destroyed their village at Tippecanoe.

This premature conflict undermined Tecumseh's plans. The following year, as the War of 1812 erupted between England and the United States, Tecumseh and the Shawnee joined the British forces. A number of Springfield settlers also participated in the fighting, including William Ward and Simon Kenton. Tecumseh was killed at the Battle of the Thames River in Canada. According to legend, Simon Kenton repaid the chief for his kindnesses to the Springfield settlers by directing Americans away from his body and disguising it so that it would not be dishonored by scalping or mutilation.

With Tecumseh's death the conflict between whites and Indians over possession of the rich and beautiful Ohio land finally ended. The settlers of Springfield lost their fear of Indian alarms and were able to enjoy a greater sense of peace and security.

2 *Old Settlers Versus the New*

With pacification, growth, and progress assured, Springfield became a flourishing town. It had eight mercantile stores and numerous mechanical shops. Extensive sheep raising by area farmers supported a woolen cloth factory. By 1818 Springfield had become the seat of a newly created county, but there was growing conflict between older and newer settlers. The carefree life of the frontiersmen clashed with efforts to establish a more civilized community.

James Demint, pioneer founder of the town, was described as a rough and fearless man, but his friends said he could be warmhearted and generous. Still others described him as a hard-drinking gambler, and a good example of all that needed improvement in his town.

Contention developed first over Muster Day. By law, able-bodied men had to attend public drill. At least two musters were held each year, during the fall and spring, in a large field west of town. Some men were members of regular units that met all year while others were put into special units just for the muster. Regular companies included the Springfield Artillery ("the best drilled and neatest equipped"), the Clark Guards, the Osceola Plaids, and the Springfield Cadets.

As the threat of Indian attacks waned, muster was taken less seriously and degenerated into an occasion for frolic and mischief. Many put off the settling of disputes, saying, "We'll settle this at muster." "Granny" Icenberger, one of the characters of the little town, appeared at every muster, selling old-fashioned ginger cake and home brew to the men and boys at camp.

In spite of the Muster Day obligations, life in the fledgling community was somewhat easygoing. Every weekend was like a holiday, and the favorite sport was horse racing. The taverns were the center of village life, places where people gathered to await the mail, to gossip, to drink rum and whiskey, and to gamble. All of these activities led to fighting and raucous behavior. An early chronicler described a typical Saturday in town: "Men met to run horses, take a spree, and wound up. . .quarreling and fighting." One participant, he continued, retired from the scene "with a gouged eye, another with a bloody nose and bruised face." The Sabbath, too, he said, was spent in vice and wickedness, yet there were "men of upright, moral, and firm character" who sought "to stem the rapid progress of iniquity."

During the winter of 1810 to 1811 there was quite a revival of religion. A number of "New Light" or Christian preachers converged on the town to conduct a "season of religious excitement." It turned a number of nonchurchgoing frontiersmen into Christians. The enthusiasm was so great that the converts built the first church in town. When it was finished, the "New Lights" offered it as a place of worship to all. Two years later the Methodists erected the town's second church.

The New Lights were not the first to bring religion to Springfield. In 1809, one year before they arrived, the Reverend Saul Henkle found his way into the frontier community. Reverend Henkle, who came from Virginia, was an ordained preacher in the Methodist Episcopal Church, a devout Christian, and an exemplary frontier citizen. He became Springfield's first permanent minister—his ministry covering twenty-eight years—and often he

Opposite
Springfield attracted settlers from various parts of the state, resulting in diversity in ethnic and religous backgrounds. This map shows land divisions, early settlements, and military posts of Ohio in the early 1800s. Courtesy, Ohio Historical Society

was the only resident pastor. While he attended to the religious needs of Springfield, he also established churches in other parts of the county. Henkle officiated at every marriage and funeral, and no one, said the townsfolk, could be married or buried without him.

Henkle also served as clerk of courts, county recorder, and state senator. In 1818 he organized the town's first temperance society and in 1822 helped organize the Clark County Bible Society. In 1829 he became editor of the area paper, the *Western Pioneer*. He helped organize volunteer fire companies. If one was looking for an example of faith and character, as well as a counterweight to the raucous behavior of the frontiersmen, the Reverend Henkle was it.

Into this village of contrasts more settlers came. Springfield was favorably located at the intersection of three major roads. A reasonably good road, developed by the army for its expeditions against the Indians, cut through the forests from Cincinnati to Springfield and on to the northwest. Another road led east to west, from Franklinton to Springfield and on, and another road cut southwest from Springfield to Dayton.

Over these roads came new settlers. Most were Southerners from Virginia and Kentucky, but others came from Pennsylvania, Maryland, and New Jersey. Englishmen, Irishmen, and Germans were among the newcomers. At first few came from New York and New England, but their number increased with the completion of the Erie Canal in 1825. The newcomers also settled in other villages that were founded nearby: Lagonda in 1800, New Carlisle in 1810, South Charleston and Lisbon in 1815, Medway in 1816, North Hampton in 1829, and Donnelsville in 1830.

Springfield's growth was characterized by the diversity in the variety of origins of its citizenry. In Springfield the Jersey men settling the Symmes Purchase met Southerners in the Virginia Military District. Connecticut farmers from the Western Reserve met New England pioneers from the lands of the Ohio Company. Pennsylvanians and settlers from Maryland were enticed beyond the rocky hills of the Seven Ranges. The settlers from these places were of varying ethnic and religious backgrounds.

In 1816 Louis Bancroft came from Massachusetts with his wife Mary, originally from New Hampshire. Bancroft established himself as one of the leading dry goods merchants in town. He later served as deputy sheriff, and as county gauger and inspector, regulating the local liquor business. In 1817 Bancroft's nineteen-year-old brother-in-law, James S. Christie, arrived from New Hampshire. Christie and his father built a large flatboat to bring thirty passengers down the Ohio to Cincinnati. In Springfield, Christie became a contractor and builder, later established a planing mill and sash factory, and ended his

career as a real estate agent and insurance salesman.

Three leading citizens who came to Springfield from New Jersey included Pierson Spining, who arrived in 1812, Samson Mason, in 1818, and William Werden, in 1819. A merchant of uncommon enterprise, Spining made regular buying trips to New York and Philadelphia, brought the goods overland to Pittsburgh, and from there took them by flatboat to Cincinnati. He dropped goods at his father's stores in Hamilton and Dayton and brought the remainder to his own store in Springfield. He sold dry goods, groceries, and iron stoves. Spining acquired a large amount of real estate and later became the chief contractor for construction of the National Road through Clark County. He brought the town's first piano from New York for his wife, and people came from miles around to see and hear it.

Samson Mason was an attorney and politician of unusual ability. Four years after his arrival he was elected prosecuting attorney. Later he became state senator and elector for Henry Clay. In 1834 he was the Whig candidate for Congress and served eight years. Mason concluded his career as a state representative, U.S. attorney for Ohio in President Millard Fillmore's administration, and Clark County's delegate to the state constitutional convention of 1850 to 1851.

William Werden became the town's most famous innkeeper. Earlier taverns, like that of Griffith Foos, were utilitarian and barely comfortable. Werden gave Springfield a first-class hotel and built a statewide reputation. He quelled the rowdyism and barroom brawling that was such a nuisance to travelers in most towns. His hotel was the stop for stagecoaches, and the Werden House sign displayed a stagecoach with horses running at full speed.

John Monahan noted that, "the stages came tearing into town and up to Uncle Billy Werden's tavern on Main Street, drawn by four horses, or six when the road was rough, and carrying from eighteen to twenty-four passengers, baggage, and mail from Vienna Crossroads, [traveling] eleven miles in fifty minutes." It was common, he continued, "to see the Werden house full to overflowing, with men sleeping all around the parlors, having paid fifty cents for the privilege of sleeping on the floor."

Werden, always a genial host, also served as postmaster during President Andrew Jackson's administration. He was one of only thirteen Democrats in town out of two hundred voters. Werden also helped organize the Episcopal Church in 1834 and supported the founding of a high school.

Representative of the Pennsylvanians who came was James L. Torbert. Torbert arrived in Ohio in 1818, fresh from Princeton College, to teach at a classical academy in Lebanon, Ohio. In 1824 he moved to Springfield and taught languages while he pursued the study of law with

Samson Mason. He then served for many years as judge of the Twelfth Judicial District and later judge of probate court. When Springfield was incorporated in 1827, Torbert was elected the town's first mayor. He was an early opponent of slavery and held to his views even in what was generally a Southern-oriented town.

Although prohibited by the Ordinance of 1787, a number of early settlers brought slaves with them. Some form of slavery existed in Ohio as late as 1830 and although there were no slave auctions, there were many who were sympathetic to the system. A house in Clifton, south of Springfield, was built by slaves in 1812. James Demint was convicted of hiring the slaves of John Kenton and paying them directly rather than negotiating their use through their owner. Tirades against abolition appeared in local papers, and those who had strong views against slavery were roughly received. Judge Torbert, however, because he was respected and well liked, was able to lay firm groundwork for those who opposed the practice.

The leading newcomer from the South was Maddox Fisher, who arrived from Kentucky in 1813. With his silver-headed cane, silver snuff box, private carriage, and footman, Fisher was the picture of a Southern aristocrat. A man of energy and ability, he brought a new spirit to the town. He also brought his accumulated assets of $20,000—a fortune in those days. Fisher bought twenty-five lots from James Demint, built a flour mill, and opened a dry goods store. Real estate had been depressed, but values moved up with Fisher's activities.

Fisher is credited with initiating the move to create Clark County from parts of Greene, Champaign, and Madison counties, and he was instrumental in getting Springfield designated as county seat in 1818. Springfield was competing for the seat with the village of New Boston, which had developed on the site of the Indian village of Piqua. Springfield was a stronghold of the Whig Party, while New Boston was a Democratic town. Fisher went to Chillicothe where the legislature was in session. A persuasive and congenial lobbyist, he enlisted a majority in support of Springfield and won by two votes. When the news reached Springfield, the citizenry assembled at a public house. They "made merry," observed a chronicler of the times, "burning tar barrels and dealing pretty freely with spirits."

Progress became more rapid after the creation of Clark County, but not all lived or stayed to see it. James Demint died in 1817, and Simon Kenton moved further north to the less-settled Zanesfield. Many of the original settlers saw little need for establishment of the county or the town's incorporation. Yet, the Southern yeomanry that made up a majority of the population took control of the county's political machinery, and a rivalry between town and county began. The rivalry was between the Demo-crats in the county and Whigs in town, and between Southern farmers and townsfolk from New England and the East.

Springfield in 1818 contained a number of brick and frame houses, but most were still made of logs. Nevertheless there were those who dreamed of better things. The beautiful rivulet, Mill Run, glided smoothly through the town, dividing it into two sections. To the west was Old Virginny, the abode of earlier settlers of Southern origin. To the east lived newcomers from the eastern states. There were few sidewalks, and the town was famous for its muddy streets. To get from the East to Old Virginny, one waded through mud and mire to a foot log, ascending and descending steep and slippery banks on the way. Many townsfolk had lobbied for incorporation in order to solve such problems. The town's more ardent advocates of progress dubbed the area where the county courthouse was built in Demint's original public square "Sleepy Hollow." They wanted to call attention to the slow, almost imperceptible pace of government affairs.

The four corner lots at Columbia and Limestone streets had been given to the town by James Demint. Since the official government was the county, it assumed jurisdiction over these commons and built the courthouse there. One of the lots was used by the farmers of the county as a place to show their horses. In true Southern style, court day and horse day were one and the same. There was always an abundance of good horses, and special attention was paid to raising fine stallions. Often more attention was paid to viewing the horses than to the business of the courthouse.

The first census of Clark County, taken in 1820, showed a population of 610: 285 males and 325 females. There were eight general stores, a flour mill, a woolen and carding mill, a cotton mill, a printing office, and a post office. There were also lumber and powder mills. The census also reported ninety-four houses in the county.

Growth and progress stopped with the Panic of 1819. The failure of the Second Bank of the United States affected the West drastically. Bankers, merchants, manufacturers, and farmers, as well as speculators, went down in the general collapse. Farm prices fell, and the nation experienced a general depression. For frontier towns like Springfield the economic effects of the Panic were felt for five full years, and only gradually did the economy pick up.

Most people had bought their land on credit. They bought 320 acres with one-fourth down and the balance due in three payments. Because of the depression, they could not sell off part to pay for the rest, and with the decline of farm prices and the failure of state currencies, they could not raise cash. Many frontiersmen who hadn't lost their land because of unclear title, lost it because they were unable to pay for it. Many moved further west to try again. The struggle between county debtors and town creditors did not help to ease the strain in relationships.

In the depths of the depression, the Second Great Awakening, a religious revival, swept through upstate New York and spread across the country. Camp meetings were held in the Springfield area on the plain above Aberfelda Ravine west of town. The first Presbyterian church had been founded in 1817, and in 1819, coinciding with the beginning of the Panic, the Associate Reform Presbyterian Church was established. (Later, Sabbath schools were introduced, and the first permanent one, apparently a cooperative venture, was started in a brick schoolhouse in 1827.) In 1824 the African Methodist Episcopal Church was organized to serve a growing black population, which numbered more than fifty. Reverend Henkle published the *Gospel Trumpet* as preachers in the area sounded the call for sinners to repent.

The U.S. Congress acted to alleviate the economic distress caused by the Panic. The Land Law of 1820 eased conditions under which new land purchases could be made. It reduced the size of the tract that an individual had to buy from 320 acres to 80 acres and fixed the price at one dollar and twenty-five cents per acre. For just $100 a man could own a farm! One year later, the Relief Act was passed to try to save those who had not already failed. It stated that if a man had bought more land than he could pay for, he could return part in lieu of further payment. For his one-quarter down, he could retain 80 acres and return 240. If he had made additional payments, he could keep 80 acres for each one. If he wanted the entire 240 acres, he could make a cash settlement at a thirty-seven-and-a-half percent discount, or he could elect to pay eight annual installments with interest remitted.

These two acts did little to recoup the fortunes of the pioneers (they had already forfeited their land and moved on), but went a long way toward solidifying the position of the farmers and newcomers. When the acts took effect, prosperity returned, and the town's growth resumed.

While Congress was creating its economic aids for Springfield and the community was experiencing the religious fervor of the Second Great Awakening, George Smith came into town with his printing press. Arriving in 1820, Smith began publishing *The Farmer,* a weekly newspaper that advocated the principles of the Madison administration. The paper was Republican during the Adams-Jackson controversy, and it remained Republican and Whig. In 1821 the paper came into the hands of the prestigious Rogers family. It was published first by Henry Rogers, second by Benjamin Rogers, who changed the name to the *Western Pioneer,* and third by Simeon Rogers. In 1825 attorney George W. Jewett became the publisher. Jewett held several political offices, including

The bell in the Clark County Courthouse was first sounded to announce a meeting in support of John Quincy Adams. Built in 1827, the courthouse was sold for fifty-five dollars in 1878 and finally razed in 1887. The courthouse is pictured circa 1876. CCHS

township trustee and prosecuting attorney. He was also vice-president of the Bible Society and an active and well-known citizen.

In 1822 the Pennsylvania House was built at the fork in the road west of town. One could now stop to rest before continuing southwest to Dayton or west to Indiana. When the traffic increased, the hotel became a major stopover for teamsters pulling loads east or west.

In 1825 the town provided street lighting. "A large glass lamp, with double reflectors," the *Western Pioneer* reported, "at a cost of about twenty-five dollars each" was placed on posts at suitable points around the town. A fee of twelve-and-a-half cents was charged each house for oil and wicks. The lamps were lit and cared for free of charge by the persons "before whose door the posts should be placed."

Finally in 1827, nine years after the townsfolk first started lobbying, the village was incorporated. Mail delivery was improved. Beginning in 1828, a four-horse coach arrived every day with news from Washington and Baltimore, just five days after its publication there. The first courthouse was built in 1827, and in 1828 a bell was placed in its cupola. Historian Robert C. Woodward stated "its long and clamorous tongue" was first used to call people to a rally in support of John Quincy Adams. Springfield politician Samson Mason addressed the gathered crowd.

This view, titled Springfield from the East, *is an etching from a Thomas Wharton drawing completed in February 1832. The growing community of Springfield is pictured emerging from the countryside. CCHS*

On September 28, 1828, the *Western Pioneer* featured a sketch of the town's development: It showed substantial growth since the 1820 census. The town's population alone was 925—300 more than the whole county eight years before. There were six blacksmith shops, four coach and wagon shops, two shops making commercial and fancy chairs, four boot and shoemakers, three tanneries, one curriery, six tailor shops, three saddle- and harness-making shops, three bakeries, three cabinet shops, one clockmaker and one watchmaker, two hatters, one coppersmith, one tin shop, two cooper shops, two millwrights, two extensive distilleries, fourteen mercantile shops, four grocers, and twenty-seven house carpenters and joiners. Together these enterprises employed 194 people.

The *Western Pioneer* continued its tally: there was an extensive flour mill, three good houses of entertainment, two schools for girls and two for boys. The town had four attorneys and five physicians. There were three butcheries, three brickyards, one gun shop, two wheelwrights, one pottery, and more bricklayers, stonemasons, and plasterers than the editor could count. In addition, there were two house and sign painters, and one "portrait, miniature, and fancy painter," an engraver, and a gilder. In many cases there were more jobs being done than the number of people doing them because some did more than one thing. The town also had a courthouse, a brick jail, two church buildings with a third in progress, and a post office.

As the town grew, the location of the market house became another issue over which town and county disagreed. A market house was important because it provid-

ed a place where area farmers could display produce and farmers and townspeople could buy or barter. A temporary market had been established on North Street in Old Virginny in 1826. It boasted such delicacies as bear meat and venison hams. The following year a new, more permanent place was built on Market Street on the east side of Mill Run. Supporters of the market in Old Virginny objected and tried to keep both going, but they failed. In 1829 proposals for a new, two-story brick market building, which would house town offices and a meeting hall, were laid before the town council. By 1832 the town opened the new market house on Market Square. The center of town was now clearly east of Mill Run and up the hill, several blocks from Demint's original town square.

The new town center lined up with the proposed route of the National Road that was to come through town. In the meantime, the town's boosters worked to move the town south a few blocks. The roadbed from Franklinton that came into Demint's original square was not to be used. Surveyors for the federal highway from Cumberland, Maryland, picked a route further south and on higher, dryer ground. By 1818 the road had reached the Ohio River, and by 1832 it was to be opened through Springfield.

Springfielders were excited. They had missed out on the canals that brought life to towns like Piqua and Dayton. Springfield was not on Ohio canal routes and many had thought they might lose their gamble on land in Clark County. The National Road would improve the east-west route, which already served the town, and enhance land values.

Pierson Spining took the contract to build the road over the strong objections of his wife, who most likely feared the risk of loss was too great. The labor was done by local workmen in Spining's employment, but army engineers were in charge. The workmen were predominantly German and Irish immigrants who were paid ninety cents a day along with jiggers of whiskey. A jigger boss was responsible for passing up and down the road during the day with a jug and pouring out to each man his hourly jigger (perhaps another reason for Mrs. Spining's dismay).

Spining did lose money on the project, primarily because of long delays, unexpected problems, and changes in the plans. Ultimately, he recouped his losses through the growing value of his extensive real estate holdings, located in the town's new center, and his mercantile pursuits. Other speculators and merchants also prospered, including Maddox Fisher, property owner and merchant. The rivalry between Fisher's store and Spining's was one of most the exciting things happening at that time in the little town. The two men were located across the street from one another and each worked to outdo the other.

Springfield was changing. The recently constructed

roads and businesses were bringing renewed prosperity to the frontier town, but it wouldn't be long before the town outgrew its frontier beginnings. In 1830 two men arrived in Springfield whose differences illustrated the transformations taking place within it. One represented the frontier life the town was leaving, and the other represented the new culture it was beginning to embrace.

The first man was Johnny Appleseed, who came along planting apple trees and visiting relatives near Chapman's Creek. He represented a free and unsettled spirit typical of the frontier. The second newcomer was Jeremiah Warder, a wealthy and cultured Quaker from Philadelphia, who came with his wife Anne Aston Warder and seven of their twelve children. These cultured Philadelphians owned extensive acreage around Springfield and were determined to build an outpost of the eastern civilization they had left behind.

Jeremiah Warder had an opportunity to purchase from his father's estate extensive land holdings his father had to the west in Ohio, including 640 acres east of Springfield. He came to evaluate the prospects and was persuaded by Griffith Foos and Maddox Fisher to move to Springfield. Warder's first experiences upon arrival were not happy ones. The work he had arranged to be done—building a home and preparing his farm—was not completed as fast or as well as he had expected. In Philadelphia it would have been different, he thought. He was also unhappy with the physicians he found. According to Warder they were well behind the times compared to doc-

Jeremiah Warder, a cultured Philadelphia Quaker who later became a highly successful businessman, arrived in Springfield in 1830. A patron of the arts, he organized the Springfield Lyceum, a literary club. This image is reproduced from a portrait by Rembrandt Peale. CCHS

Anne Aston Warder, wife of Jeremiah Warder, came to Springfield with her husband and seven of their twelve children. As they took up residence they vowed to devote their energies and those of their children to raising the quality of life in Springfield. This image is reproduced from a portrait by Rembrandt Peale. CCHS

tors in the East. Writing to one of his friends back East, he implied that there were no doctors in Springfield. He added that he hoped the pioneers would move further west and that their places would be taken by others of more civilized habits of work and behavior.

Springfield was not as devoid of civilization as Warder's letters home seemed to suggest. Many efforts had been made to create literary and benevolent societies: a literary society was formed in 1815, a library society in 1816, another library society in 1820, a Bible society in 1822, and a missionary society in 1826. In 1826 a society for the encouragement of instrumental music was founded, and in 1827 a vocal music society came into being. In 1828 another literary society was attempted, and in 1829 a reading room society and a temperance society emerged. Most such efforts, however, could not be sustained, and while the aspirations were there, more was needed to make life in the town as culturally satisfying as some wished it to be.

There were positive signs. In 1830 John D. Nichols, an itinerant bookseller from Massachusetts, settled in Springfield and opened the town's first bookstore. He brought a

stock of books and stationery from Cincinnati, shipping them by canal to Dayton and bringing them the rest of the way by wagon. His store became an information center. He offered such early specials as *History of All Religions* and *Butler's Universal History.* He published several works himself, including *Life of General Jackson* and the *Western Medical Journal.*

Yet there were other signs, too, that indicated Springfield had more work to do to shake its still-frontier stereotype. In 1830 a group of interested Springfielders offered the Ohio Baptist Society a quarter section of land (160 acres) if it agreed to build its proposed college in Springfield. The society decided, however, to build in the more isolated village of Granville so that students might be protected from the evil influences of frontier society.

For some their task in Springfield was apparent. Jeremiah and Anne Aston Warder, in particular, were determined to improve life and raise the level of civilization in Springfield. As they took up residence, they vowed to devote their energies and those of their children to that end.

Latest Arrival from Philadelphia!

SECOND SUPPLY AT THE

BEE- HIVE!

BEAN & GRIGGS

HAVE THIS DAY, (NOV. 27,) RECEIVED A SECOND SUPPLY OF

FALL AND WINTER

GOODS!

THEIR ASSORTMENT OF

DRY GOODS,

GROCERIES,

QUEENSWARE AND HARDWARE,

BOOTS AND SHOES,

CAPS AND BONNETS,

IS LARGER, BETTER, AND CHEAPER THAN EVER.

We would again renew our solicitations for the continuance of that patronage so liberally extended to us, and invite our friends and customers to call and examine our stock before purchasing. Our stock was bought at *Cash Prices*, and will be sold *Cheap for Cash*, or Prompt Pay.   BEAN & GRIGGS.

N. B.---Beeswax, Honey, Rags, Feathers, Tallow, Butter, Lard, Soap, Cheese, Eggs, Linsey, Clover, Flax and Timothy Seed, wanted in any quantity at the BEE-HIVE.   B. & G.

SPRINGFIELD, Nov. 27, 1845.

GALLAGHER & CRAIN, Printers, Springfield, Ohio.

3 Civil War Boomtown

In 1830 Springfield was still a village lost in the Ohio forest, as one stagecoach passenger described it. All the habitations through which he had traveled for several days and nights "were as nothing compared with the forests."

Thirty years later, however, the village would be a town, the forest gone, and Ohio would rank third among the states in population and wealth. In 1830 Springfield had a population of 1,080; by 1860 its population would pass 7,000 and Clark County would boast over 22,000 residents. The frontier was passing, and a bustling industrial center was emerging.

Jeremiah Warder played a major role in that transition. Together with his wife Anne, Warder brought to Springfield a commitment to good causes and interest in the improvement of society to local affairs. Though they ceased to be active Quakers, their contributions were marked by Quaker traits. Warder built a house on a road leading east from town, which he named High Street in good English fashion. It was the high street coming into the newly relocated Market Square, and it became Springfield's first fashionable street.

As the area was developed, citizens called it Prospect Heights because of the beautiful view of the surrounding country which was obtained from the High Street hill. It was one of the greatest attractions of the town, observed one citizen, with a fine view of the village and the Buck Creek Valley. It was a favorite promenade of the "swains and lassies" of the day.

Warder got his farms into production, fencing in his fields in an uncharacteristic fashion for the frontier. Up until then everyone figured it was sufficient to simply *know* where the boundaries were. What livestock there was roamed fairly freely. Warder also encouraged friends and acquaintances from the East to move to the village.

At his insistence, Dr. Robert Rodgers came to Springfield in 1832 at the age of twenty-five and becam a major community contributor. Rodgers had been previously settled in Portsmouth after finishing medical studies at the University of Pennsylvania, until Warder talked him into moving. When he arrived he set up his practice and remained there until he was seventy-three. Rodgers performed the first Caesarean operation in the county. In order to set a higher standard for medical practice, he led efforts to found the Clark County Medical Society in 1838. Rodgers also persuaded his brother William to move to Springfield, and William became a very successful banker.

Families such as the Brains and Wheldons, who had moved to Philadelphia from England, also took Warder's advice and moved to Springfield. George Brain bought 160 acres at seven dollars an acre, to which he later added another 190 acres. Joseph Wheldon bought a sizable farm near the Brains and built a twelve-room house. A Wheldon daughter, Mary, later married one of the Warder sons.

Isaac Ward, Dr. Rodger's brother-in-law, came also. He purchased a large tract of land north of Buck Creek, which included the original site of James Demint's cabin. He built a home that still stands as part of the Ward-Frey-Gano house on North Fountain Avenue.

Opposite
Merchants Bean and Griggs announced the arrival of a second shipment of goods from Philadelphia on November 27, 1845. They were ready to sell "cheap for cash or prompt pay" various "drygoods, groceries, queensware, boots and shoes, caps, and bonnets" and "wanted in any quantity" "beeswax, honey, rags, feathers, tallow, butter, lard, soap, cheese, eggs, linsey, clover, flax, and Timothy seed." CCHS

Jeremiah Warder purchased the *Western Pioneer* and turned it over to newcomers Edward H. Cummings and John M. Gallagher. Both became longtime contributors to the town's educational and cultural institutions. Cummings married Warder's daughter Sarah. He was a charter member of the Episcopal Church and later became the Episcopal rector. He was also active as an officer in the local militia, which replaced the raucous muster, and for a time served as mayor.

Cummings helped organize Springfield High School, founded in 1834. The high school was operated by Principal Milo G. Williams as a private preparatory school where students also received their first two years of college education. In 1842 operation of the school was transferred to the Ohio Conference of the Methodist Episcopal Church. Cummings was also instrumental in establishing the Clark County Agricultural Society in 1840, which was designed to improve the standards of farming.

Gallagher contributed to the organization of the high school and the agricultural society, and helped organize the First Baptist Church and the Springfield Lyceum. He was elected to the state legislature, where he served as speaker of the house. Above all, however, Gallagher operated the newspaper. He used it to emphasize community pride and progress, in his view the highest purpose to which a newspaper could be devoted.

Springfield was moving toward improvement. The newspaper, high school, churches, lyceum, medical society, and agricultural society were proof of it, and the *Western Pioneer* recorded every development. Warder was pleased with the increase in reading. Springfielders kept track of the river news in the *Cincinnati Inquirer,* and the mushy serial stories were read with great enthusiasm. More substantial fare, found at the local bookshop of Whiting and Kilbourne, was enjoyed, too. People eagerly read Charles Dickens' *Nicholas Nickleby* and James Fenimore Cooper's *The Pathfinder.*

In the 1840s one writer described the differences he observed in the town:

The primitive modes of life, the uncouth, uncultured manners of the pioneers disappeared with the forests and were replaced with a higher regard for morals and a stricter observance of the Sabbath. Brawls were less frequent; dress and behavior were higher toned; and there was a greater appreciation of learning and literature, and an awakened interest in the outside world. Men began to read and think more; and the prosperity of the future also began to be assured.

Warder helped to stimulate the town's economic and industrial prosperity. In 1830 he purchased the village of Lagonda and the mills started by Springfield trailblazer

Simon Kenton and immediately improved their efficiency. Other needs, however, had to be met before much economic progress could be made.

The development of roads and turnpikes was a first step. With the opening of the National Road in 1832, Springfield became even more the crossroads of a westward-moving nation. Hundreds of wagons and stagecoaches connected in Springfield. In 1836 the *Western Pioneer* reported that 1,200 Conestoga wagons passed through town during September and October. By 1848, when the Mad River and Lake Erie Railroad was completed, the town averaged several trains and seventy-five to one hundred stagecoaches per day. The stage yards accommodated two acres of coaches and five hundred horses. David West began manufacturing buggies, and later James Driscoll opened a shop to make carriages and wagons. The liveries boomed. The local haymarket was busy and prosperous.

When federal construction of the National Road ceased in 1836, Springfield became the town at the end of the road where the westward-moving tarried, deciding how to proceed. Many stayed and the town's population increased. As a result, Springfield became a great hotel town. On East Main Street there was the United States Hotel, a "movers' tavern" with a large yard to accommodate covered wagons. At Main and Center streets there were two more movers' taverns—the American and the Western, plus the Murray House two blocks east. Further west on Main Street was the Pennsylvania House. Pierson Spining opened the Buckeye House at Main and Limestone streets. This hotel was built around an open courtyard, and the rooms opened onto galleries (extended porches) where guests could congregate for socializing. There was also Werden's famous National Hotel, formerly known as Werden House, at Main and Spring streets.

Federal crews built bridges west of town and carved the hills through which the roadbed for the National Road was to go. They filled in large portions of Aberfelda Ravine and graded the roadbed for several miles. Other roads led from Springfield south and north and then west.

With transportation provided for, the enterprising turned their attention increasingly to energy sources. James Leffel, a resident tinkerer and inventor, led the way. In 1840 Leffel built a foundry on Buck Creek, west of town. While engaged in the foundry business, he experimented with a variety of ideas. His neighbors described him as blessed with a seemingly inexhaustible supply of energy.

Leffel believed that the water in Buck Creek could be used as a power source for the city. He proposed bringing a portion of the creek in a race down the north side of its banks to the foot of Limestone Street. Though his idea was hotly debated by everyone in town he persuaded the

James Leffel, foundry owner and inventor, proposed building Spring-field's mill race in 1841. The one-and-a-half-mile race drove twenty water wheels. In 1862 Leffel was granted a patent on his double-turbine water wheel. CCHS

Barnett brothers, local manufacturers, of the plan's utility. In 1841, on land purchased from Joseph Perrin, Richard Rodgers, and Jeremiah Warder, Leffel and the Barnetts constructed a one-and-a-half-mile race with a fall of twenty-four feet, developing enough water power to propel twenty wheels. The results were so effective, and so much power was generated, that Springfield manufacturers ignored the steam engine for many years.

From the Mill Race came power for a dozen new factories. A cotton mill, three woolen mills, an oil mill, two flouring mills, two sawmills, and other plants were set up at the northern edge of town. There James S. Christie and Lucius Muzzy built their planing mill and sash factory, and Hatch and Whitely built their foundry.

The earliest boom industry was the woolen mills. Jeremiah Warder's major enterprise became the Warder and McLaughlin Woolen Mill. McLaughlin was one of many master mechanic craftsmen who passed through town. By 1847 John and William Ramsey founded their woolen mills on Mill Run, and that same year Charles Rabbitts picked Springfield for the location of his mill. He cited three reasons for bringing the enterprise to town: cheap water power, railroads, and the town and its people.

This new mill gave Springfield its fifth woolen mill. Farmers brought wool from more than twenty miles away. At first they brought it to be carded and took it home to spin and weave, bringing back flannel to be finished. Later they sold wool directly, and the mills made cloth and

kept it in stock to barter for raw wool. The industry grew, making yarns, flannels, blankets, cloth, satinettes, and jeans.

In the 1850s two new industrialists, the young Phinias P. Mast and John H. Thomas, were attracted by the cheap energy that the mill owners had tapped. They purchased a building on the north side of Buck Creek where Dr. T.J. Kindleburger, another of the area's inventors, had worked. There they manufactured cider presses and grain drills. The presses sold well, making enough money for the two of them to continue improvement of their drills. While the town's leaders continued to update and expand energy resources, with new entrepreneurs frequently joining them, experimentation began in the manufacture of farm machinery. William Whitely started making plows in 1840, and John Pitts began making threshing machines in 1842.

As the town grew in size the need for cooperative community efforts also grew. The need to work together was nowhere more apparent than in firefighting. The earliest volunteer fire companies were informal groups of citizens who agreed to protect one another's property. By 1837 the Utilities organized as the first formal volunteer fire company. They were joined in 1838 by the Independents. The two groups were social clubs as much as they were fire companies, and as their members aged the groups faltered.

In 1853 the Utilities disbanded and were succeeded by a group of younger men, the Neptunes. In 1854 the Independents disbanded and were succeeded by the Rovers. Spirited rivalry developed between the two new groups. They raced to fires to see who could get there first. Even small fires received attention from both groups. It was considered a disgrace to go to a fire and not put a stream of water on it. Often more damage was done by excessive water than by the fire itself. Nevertheless, getting a stream of water on a fire was difficult, and the young men were encouraged to lay the hose from creek to fire—thousands of feet—and to get the water flowing everywhere they could in anticipation of the day it would be needed.

That day came in February 1841, when the town suffered the largest fire loss in its young history. A livery stable in Primrose Alley caught fire, and the fire spread rapidly to the Republic Building on Main Street where the town newspaper was published. East of the Republic was a brand new, three-story business complex, the Linn Building, part of the finest business block in town. It was completely destroyed. Two smaller buildings were also engulfed, and the Fisher Building was slightly damaged. Across the street sparks ignited the Murray House and destroyed it.

The two fire companies, with their old, double-decked, Philadelphia engines, did the best they could, pumping water 2,000 feet from source to fire, but it was hard to get

a heavy flow, and the wind from the west was strong. The gathered crowd expected the whole eastern part of town to burn, but when the eastern wall of the Murray House held, the fire was contained in the two blocks already ablaze. By midnight the fire was under control.

In the aftermath residents looked for a cause. According to one theory some men were playing cards, gambling in the haymow of a livery stable, and upset a lantern that set fire to the hay. Others thought the town's great disaster was caused by boys who were staging a cockfight in a packing house. No one was ever able to decide where or how the fire actually started, but residents were convinced that it was caused by either the immoral behavior of gamblers or cockfighters.

. The need for a cooperative effort was also apparent in weather disasters and epidemics of disease. Early in 1832 torrential rains drenched the area, and Mad River, living up to its name, flooded its banks half-a-mile wide. Streams were higher than they had been in twenty years, and farmers spent months repairing damages.

That winter cholera (often called immigrant fever) came into the area. Springfield escaped the full horrors, but there were thirty-three deaths in New Carlisle. Authorities in Springfield proposed extraordinary measures, and the people agreed. A citizens meeting passed resolutions requesting the council to enforce all sanitary ordinances, to clean and purify streets and alleys, and to divide the town into four districts. A sanitary committee was formed in each district, and the committee members inspected the area and enforced the law. When the threat passed and the town was left virtually untouched, residents were proud of their efforts.

In 1849 the cholera returned. As the railroad was being built west of town, a large company of Irish workers were making the land cut. Cholera broke out among them, and over fifty died. They were to be buried in the Catholic cemetery east of town, but city authorities objected to their bodies being taken through town during the busy daylight hours. The undertaker later had to transport them all at night when people were safely inside their homes.

The citizenry became better organized to provide help when the town was incorporated as a city. Springfield Senator Harvey Vinal introduced the bill to incorporate the city, and it passed the legislature on March 21, 1850.

Opposite, left
Phineas P. Mast began production of farm equipment during the 1850s and was a leader in Springfield's industrialization. CCHS

Opposite, right
James M. Hunt was elected the first mayor of the newly incorporated City of Springfield in 1850. CCHS

In a referendum in May the town voted to accept incorporation, 386 to 63. James M. Hunt, a local attorney, was elected the first mayor. Councilmen elected were Alexander Ramsey, John C. Filler, C.D. McLaughlin, Harvey Vinal, John Householder, and Daniel von Huben. Martin Carey was elected town marshal.

As soon as the city was incorporated, it enacted ordinances to eliminate unsanitary waste disposal and unruly behavior and drunkenness, and to control animals within the city limits. It provided for better streets and required every citizen to work two days a year on city streets and roads.

In 1850 Springfield also received gas lights. The Springfield Gas and Coke Company set up six street lights, piped gas to several stores, and installed eighteen burners in city hall. Officers and directors of the company included Charles Anthony, president; James S. Goode, secretary; and William Foos, Peter Murray, T.J. Kindleburger, and Joshua Gore.

The churches provided help to their members, and there were growing numbers of interdenominational activities, particularly among the women. Women were the most active members of the local chapter of the American Bible Society. Nevertheless, the reports were given by men at the annual meetings.

Additional fire-fighting companies were also founded, as well as fraternal orders like the Masons and the Odd Fellows. The first Odd Fellows Lodge formed on October 24, 1844. Clark Lodge of Free and Accepted Masons started in February 1848. In 1850 the Masons and Odd Fellows built Union Hall, which housed businesses on the first floor and meeting rooms on the second. When the town's first Jewish synagogue was organized, it used the hall as its place of worship. The Holy Congregation of Benevolent Men was served by Rabbi Myers in 1868 and grew to forty members.

Jeremiah Warder could be proud of the progress Springfield had made. He died in 1849, and his widow survived him for two decades. A quiet leader, she became affectionately known as Mother Warder. Together the two Warders contributed greatly to Springfield's community spirit, and several of their children made major contributions to the town as well. William Warder operated the Warder and Burnett Flour Mills, J. Thompson Warder operated and developed the original Warder farm east of town, and Benjamin Head Warder operated the gristmills and sawmills at Lagonda.

This was an era when men worked by the day at what was known as a steady scale, a set pay per day regardless of hours worked. From September 20 to January 20, they worked an eight-and-a-half-hour day; from January 20 to May 20, a ten-hour day; and from May 20 to September 20, from ten-and-a-half to eleven-and-a-half hours a day.

29

Above
Benjamin H. Warder, son of Jeremiah and Anne Aston Warder, operated the gristmills and sawmills at Lagonda. Warder is pictured circa 1870. Courtesy, Warder Memorial Library

Top, left
Charles Anthony, pictured circa 1850, was president of the Springfield Gas and Coke Company, which set up six streetlights and installed eighteen burners in City Hall in 1850. Five years earlier Anthony had also been instrumental in convincing the founding fathers of Wittenberg to locate their college in Springfield. Courtesy, Warder Memorial Library

Left
Ezra Keller came from Baltimore to organize Wittenberg College. The first classes were held on November 3, 1845, on the ground floor of the First Lutheran Church at the corner of what is now Wittenberg Avenue and High Street. From the Wittenberg University Archives

The system was an outgrowth of work on the farm. The workday grew longer as the days grew longer, and shorter as daylight hours diminished. Around 1849, when the ten-hour workday legislation began to have impact, employers shifted to the new system. At John Pitts' thresher works, the ten-hour day was combined with an hourly wage in place of the steady scale. Gradually more employers shifted to the hourly rate.

The change highlighted other differences between life on the farm and in the factory. The place where change became most apparent for workman and employer alike was in the emerging cycle of boom and bust. The first general economic crisis had been that of 1819 when the nation's land speculation collapsed. A second was the

Panic of 1837 following Andrew Jackson's efforts to halt inflation and preserve monetary values. In 1857 there was a third economic crisis, brought on by the over-building of railroads. Furniture-maker Peter A. Schindler told of one of the effects of the 1857 Panic:

We were running that shop during the Panic of 1857 when there was hardly any money in town, and what was here nobody felt right sure that it was worth more than fifty, sixty cents on the dollar. We could only give our employees a dollar or maybe a half-dollar each, giving them the rest of their wages in store orders.

During the Panic of 1857 there was an effort to break Springfield's first bank—the Mad River Branch of the State Bank, founded in 1847. Banks could be broken by money speculators who acquired the paper of a bank and presented it for redemption in gold. Rumors grew that a group was collecting Mad River bank notes and planning to come after the town's meager supply of gold and silver. A group of citizens, determined that the bank should not be raided, put a bucket of tar, some pillow feathers, and a rough-hewn rail in front of the bank. Inside they put a big horn, a blast from which would bring men running. When the bank brokers arrived, they were alarmed by the vigilant atmosphere and left in haste.

Yet despite the economic setbacks caused by the panics, the efforts to promote growth in Springfield were so diverse that little permanent damage was done. Local boosters continued to improve educational opportunity on the assumption that it enhanced the area's attractiveness. In 1844 the Reverend Ezra Keller arrived to consider establishing a Lutheran college in town. He wanted a site that was centrally located and accessible to major transportation routes. He was interested in Columbus, Springfield, Dayton, and Xenia. By visiting each city he hoped to encourage resident support for the college.

Springfielders, however, seemed disinterested. When an open meeting was called for the Associate Reformed Church to discuss the value of securing the college for Springfield the turnout was less than hoped for and the meeting was adjourned. Editor John M. Gallagher of *The Springfield Republic,* the former *Western Pioneer,* expressed fear that the village would become a byword for the want of spirit and enterprise. He told Springfielders that the college would have moral, intellectual, and economic advantages. "Every foot of real estate within some miles," he advised, "will be more or less enhanced in value."

At a second meeting attendance was better. Springfielders had learned that Xenia was also interested in securing the college. Keller discussed the college, its advantages and prospects. He said it would benefit the county in general and the German population in par-

ticular. William A. Rodgers, the prominent banker, introduced resolutions to approve the charter of the college, ask that it be located in Springfield, and solicit subscriptions for its support. All passed unanimously.

In February 1845 a committee made up of Rodgers, Charles Anthony, Edward Swope, and Daniel von Huben presented the town's case to the board of directors of the future Wittenberg College. It was succinct: Springfield's support of education, its reputation for good moral conduct, its history of good health, its easy access by road and railroad, and its supply of stone, lime, and lumber for building made it very attractive. Add to that the beauty of the two proposed sites, good water, and fresh air, and the four-member committee was sure the board would choose Springfield.

The proposed sites were an eight-acre plot east of town between National (Cumberland) and Lagonda roads, a part of Warder's holdings, and seventeen acres north of Buck Creek, which were owned by a cemetery association and adjoined Isaac Ward's farm. The Wittenberg Board also had a proposal from Xenia that offered $4,281 in cash and a choice of five plots. Springfield offered $4,667 and a choice of two plots. On February 17, 1845, the board inspected the sites and voted to accept Springfield's offer and chose the site owned by the cemetery association as the home for the college.

Soon thereafter Wittenberg classes began on the ground floor of the First Lutheran Church on High Street. Among the first students were a dozen young men from the community. In 1851 the college held its first graduation exercises in the town hall. A local youth, John Mitchell, was valedictorian.

A female seminary was located in Springfield in the fall of 1848 by the Miami Presbytery of the Presbyterian Church. The school started under the direction of the Reverend J.F. Sawyer. In February 1849 the Reverend Jonathan Edwards took charge. The school's board purchased a site from Dr. William A. Rodgers on the north side of Buck Creek for the erection of a building a short distance from Wittenberg.

A variety of national issues intruded on the routine concerns of area residents. Abolition, the Mexican War, the issue of slavery in the western territories, and the rising flood of immigrants crowded into the local consciousness with a new urgency. The Reverend Ezra Keller provided moral and political leadership for many area residents as he wrestled with the issue of slavery. He abhorred it but could not accept the tactics of abolitionists. The coming of the Mexican War gave better focus to Keller's thoughts. The power of the slave owner, he insisted, undermined the North and destroyed freedom. This unjust war would result in an expansion of slavery and thus had to be opposed. Five Ohio congressmen voted

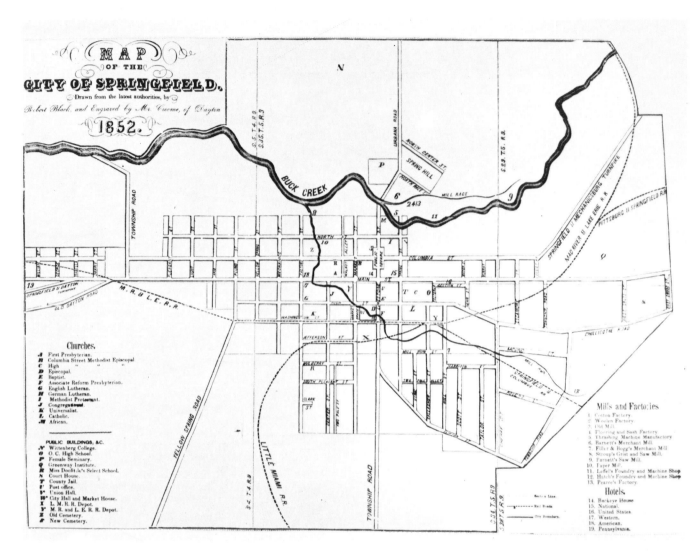

The 1852 Springfield City Directory included this map, which showed Springfield bounded on the north by North Street, on the south by Clifton Street. to the west by Pleasant Street, and to the east by Sycamore and Cherry streets. Mill Run is seen as an open stream. Courtesy, Warder Memorial Library

against the Mexican War, and Wittenberg and Springfield were centers of antiwar sentiment.

In 1842 Springfielders were not in favor of abolitionism. Chauncy Paul, a dairyman, had been tarred and feathered for an abolitionist speech in Springfield High. They stoned the school, threw eggs at the speaker, and rode him out of town on a rail. The Mexican War, however, strengthened the Free Soil Movement, which was a compromise between preserving slavery and abolishing it. It maintained that the nation might leave slavery undisturbed in the South where it already existed, but would prohibit its extension into new western territories—proclaiming them instead as free soil. It was opposed by

Southern advocates of the institution of slavery because in the long run it strengthened abolition. Every free soil territory that subsequently became a state added antislavery representatives to the United States Congress. It would then only be a matter of time until there would be enough votes in Congress to amend the Constitution to outlaw slavery everywhere.

The editor of The Springfield Republic observed that the movement was advancing rapidly. A Free Soil League was formed, and in the vanguard of the movement was William A. Rodgers, who became its unsuccessful candidate for Congress. Joshua R. Giddings, former Whig and national leader of antislavery forces, spoke twice in Springfield, hoping to arouse greater free soil sentiment. If Springfielders were lukewarm about abolition, he would enlist them for free soil in the territories.

The passage of the Kansas-Nebraska Act in 1854 opened the West to slavery, repealed the Missouri Compromise, and led to bloody conflicts between proslavery and free soil settlers. The events disturbed Springfielders, and they called upon local politician Samuel Shellabarger to review events for them. Only a free and enlightened people with a free press and a Christian spirit could preserve the nation, Shellabarger told them, and that meant that slavery and ignorance and all that sustained them had to be opposed.

Americans were distressed not only about slavery but also about immigration. In Cincinnati, Columbus, and the Northeast there were disturbances and riots. For example, during Cincinnati's spring election of 1854, nativists stole ballot boxes from German neighborhoods. In other cities Catholics were attacked and churches burned. The anti-Catholic Know Nothing party, made up of secret lodges, claimed 50,000 members in Ohio in 1854. A year later the number reached 120,000; and before the year's end it totaled 500,000. The party held a national convention in Cincinnati in November—the first political party convention held in the history of the United States.

In Springfield the Know Nothing party never even received ten percent of the vote. There were several reasons the Know Nothings gained little ground in Springfield. Area residents were well acquainted with immigrants because of railroad and road projects that had attracted Irish and Germans. The Americanization of both groups was going well. Locally, Wittenberg College, founded by German Lutherans, was considered an American institution, and Ohio nativism was more anti-Catholic and anti-foreign than anti-Lutheran. In addition, Springfield was such a melting pot of citizens of diverse origins that differences were more readily taken in stride than elsewhere.

What had a greater impact on the area was the fugitive slave law and the underground railroad. Under the fugitive slave law, residents in the North were required to return escaped slaves to bondage. Sentiment against the law grew. With the strong support of Anne Aston Warder, the Springfield Underground Railroad Association was organized, in spite of the law, to aid fugitives. White members were Mrs. Warder; Charles Stout, a livery man; Chauncy Paul, who operated a dairy and had already suffered violence for abolitionist views; John D. Nichols, editor of *The Springfield Republic;* E.A. Neff; John Courson, a tailor; Alex Cole, conductor on the Little Miami Railroad, and Mrs. Cole; George W. Cheney, conductor on the Delaware Railroad; Samuel Smith, a tanner; Christopher Thompson, a stonemason; Joshua Boucher, a preacher; M.S. Steele, a grocer; and D.S. Morrow, a tobacconist, who served as treasurer. Black members included Robert Piles, a barber, and his wife; and Mrs. Dungan and her son, George, a hotel porter.

The Springfield group was an important one because the town was important as a crossroad. There were additional stations at Mechanicsburg, Ohio, and at Selma in the southeastern part of the county. Selma was a Hicksite-Quaker community and one of the main stations for the underground railroad. Hicksite Quakers were strongly opposed to slavery and considered helping blacks to escape a Christian obligation (although a violation of the law). From Selma the fugitives were routed through Springfield, Mechanicsburg, or Marysville.

In 1857 the fugitive slave Addison White was seized by federal marshals at a farm near Mechanicsburg. Local law officials were badly treated by the marshalls. One was even beaten when he tried to stop them from returning White to the South. The slave was seized and rushed back before legal processes could be followed. The marshals' actions angered residents. They mounted a posse in pursuit, released the fugitive, and arrested the marshals. The incident caused widespread repercussions, and antislavery and anti-Southern feelings grew stronger.

During this time the area's black population noted little change in its status. In 1852 the city's first directory listed fourty-two *persons of color* who were heads of households or in business. Among the men listed were twelve laborers, six barbers, four draymen, two farmers, two whitewashers, two blacksmiths, one cook, one moulder, and one preacher, the Reverend Jeremiah Thomas. Among black women listed were nine who took in boarders, one dressmaker, and one washwoman. The number of blacks who were employed as domestics was not indicated.

The increasing antislavery sentiment prompted Samuel Shellabarger to run for Congress in 1860 on the Republican ticket. He represented the Free Soil movement and had the confidence of the town's industrial leaders, who saw the future in terms of industry, railroads, and the telegraph.

Shellabarger defeated Democrat John Scott Harrison, the eldest son of former President William Henry Harrison. The victory celebration was spectacular. Tuttle's National Silver Band played music among Roman candles, the rockets' red glare, and the sputtering of fireworks. The Wide Awakes, a band of gaily dressed crowd-rousers, paraded around the town, ending their march at the market house, where General Samson Mason, a member of the Ohio National Guard, introduced the congressman-elect.

The sounds were also those of war. Abraham Lincoln was elected president in November and by the spring of 1861 North and South were drifting toward war. On April 12, Fort Sumter was bombarded, and the Civil War began. Three days later Lincoln called for 75,000 men. In May he asked for another 60,000. Finally, on July 4, Congress was called into special session.

Springfielders responded rapidly to Lincoln's call for troops. As soon as the proclamation arrived, a town meeting was held in city hall. There was "a unanimous sentiment and a hearty endorsement" of Lincoln's position. The city's quota of troops was filled rapidly. On April 17, the Springfield Zouaves filled their ranks; by April 22, the Washington Artillery was fully enlisted and ready to go; and by April 26, the third unit, the Jefferson Guards, was ready to be commissioned. Eventually 1,243 Springfielders enlisted from a total population of 6,745. Three-fourths of the eligible men, including half of the voters, were in the service.

Reflecting hometown views, Shellabarger voted to approve the President's actions. His first important speech in the House was a defense of Lincoln's suspension of the writ of habeas corpus. He called for "almost unlimited confidence" in the President. For Ohioans the outcome of the first battles was discouraging. Twice Shellabarger had to defend the bravery of Ohio troops as federal forces lost their first encounters with the Confederates at Bull Run and won Shiloh only at great cost.

Springfielders followed the war through newspaper and telegraph. The telegraph office was located above the post office in the King Building, and the newspaper stand was in the lobby. When out-of-town papers arrived in the morning after a major battle, the lobby was jammed. Citizens waited for bulletins at the telegraph office.

The post office became popular for another reason. When war broke out, silver and gold disappeared. People used postage stamps as coinage until they were so worn the denomination could not be determined. Finally all the stamps were redeemed by the government with postal currency called "shin plasters," which served as small change for the duration. People evidently considered them similar to a type of wound patch used at the time for leg injuries.

Hardships were great for those whose men were in the army. Societies were organized to minister to their needs, and volunteers supplied food. The fraternal orders, whose membership burgeoned, also provided for the families of "brothers" in the service. The winter of 1863 was especially cold, and on December 31, farmers sent 147 wagon loads of wood to town for those whose men were at war. Colonel Peter Sintz was grand marshal, and Krapp's brass band led the way. The ten-block-long procession moved about the town dropping wood off at appropriate homes. After the distribution the donors were given a sumptuous dinner. The next day a "saw-buckeye" brigade of boys chopped the wood into smaller sizes.

The women of Springfield worked through church Ladies Aid societies and the interdenominational Soldiers Aid Society. They prepared banquets at city hall for soldiers leaving town or home on furlough and made flags, street decorations, and badges for patriotic occasions and victory celebrations. They also rolled bandages and made up packages for soldiers in camp.

The war came close to Springfield on two occasions.

On August 29, 1862, Kirby Smith's Confederate troops defeated Union forces at Richmond, Kentucky, and Ohioans feared an attack on Cincinnati. Governor David Tod called for volunteers to defend the city. Nearly 500 Clark Countians joined thousands of others in response. Shotguns and squirrel guns were the most common weapons, giving Ohio's minutemen of the Civil War the nickname of the "squirrel hunters." So many left town for Cincinnati that when a big fire broke out at Thomas Burnett's mill there were not enough men left to drag the fire engines to the fire. Burning wheat made a smoke so black and thick that it looked like the town had been bombarded. The mill was virtually destroyed.

The attack by Kirby Smith at Cincinnati never materialized, but in July 1863 Ohio was invaded by General John Morgan. Morgan's raid across the southern counties came within fifty miles of Springfield when the dashing cavalry commander took his 2,400 men across the southern part of the state. The raid was so rapid no one could respond effectively, but the remnant of the troop was captured on July 26 at Salineville in Columbiana County.

Before the war ended there was a total of thirty-four companies of volunteers of Clark County men, plus men in the regular army and navy and in the regiments of other states. Black units included the Fifth United States Colored Regiment and the Duquesne Blues, an unattached black regiment.

Hundreds were wounded and many died. Few were returned for burial. As a result Clark County soldiers are buried throughout the southern states. The first soldier buried in Ferncliff Cemetery was Patrick McKenna of the 17th Ohio Volunteers. The new cemetery was built August 25, 1863. The grounds were dedicated on the Fourth of July, 1864, by President Sprecher of Wittenberg, along with various clergy and civic leaders. Indian Hill Knoll was set apart for soldiers.

Throughout the war, efforts were made to keep spirits high, but as early enthusiasm vanished, all looked forward to the end. The news of Lee's surrender arrived on April 9. By proclamation of the governor, Springfielders celebrated the victory on April 14, 1865. According to Governor George K. Nash 5,000 gathered for the occasion. "Upon every house, upon every shop, upon every available spot," he said, "was displayed the flag of our country." Parades, fireworks, and worship services were part of the celebrations.

The news of Lincoln's assassination came the next morning. On every street corner citizens gathered to share shock and disbelief. People flocked to the post office to await the papers, and businesses remained closed. A town meeting was held in city hall. The assembly opened with prayer, and afterward the entire audience sat in silence for fifteen minutes before anyone spoke. On Sunday

When volunteers were called to defend Cincinnati against Rebel raiders during the Civil War, 500 Clark Countians responded. These minutemen of 1862 became known as "the Squirrel Hunters." This particular group of hunters participated in the First Interstate Shotgun Wing-Shooting Tournament of the National Gun Association, held near Springfield in 1885. Photo by George A. Warder, CCHS

churches were draped in mourning and funeral discourses were delivered from every pulpit.

The most lasting impact of the war was economic. War tariffs, financing of the war, liberal land policies, federal railroad policy, and federal contracts all had their effects and accentuated industrial growth. The first industry to experience war's prosperity was that of linseed oil. Foreign oil was shut out, and government demand increased rapidly. The farmer received one dollar for a bushel of flaxseed. Out of a 100 bushels of seed, millers could press two tons of oil cake and 2,000 gallons of oil. The price of oil cake rose from ten dollars to seventy dollars, and the oil brought a dollar twenty-five a gallon. Profits were substantial.

Woolen mills also prospered. Wholesale clothiers in Cincinnati contracted to make army garments, then commissioned area mills to produce the cloth. Charles Rabbitts' first order was for 10,000 yards at seventy-five cents a yard. Demand continued to expand, and area mills prospered. Rabbitts' mill made jeans cloth until 1874, when the industry moved west. Other mills made every-

thing from cloth to carpets to meet wartime demands. As a result local farmers expanded their production of flax and wool.

William Whitely and other manufacturers of farm implements found a lucrative business making army supply and forage wagons. They began to feel the demand for better machinery from farmers whose businesses were growing and who faced a shortage of hands, making machinery necessary. Springfield's implement manufacturers accumulated their profits as a base for postwar expansion while addressing the farmer's needs for improved plows, threshers, and harvesters.

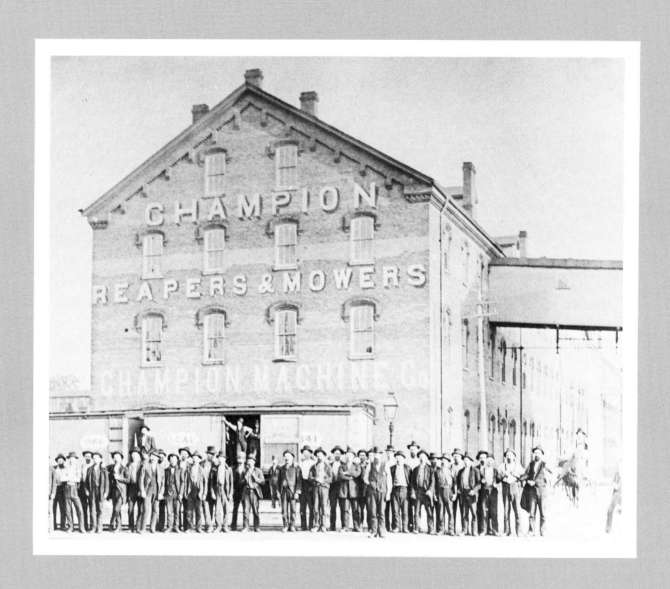

4 *The Champion City*

Springfielders sought a suitable monument to the gallant soldiers who had helped preserve the nation. The monument selected was a statue of a young man, clad in the uniform most familiar locally, a machine-made uniform that could well have been constructed from Springfield jeans. The pose was that of a soldier at parade rest.

When the statue was dedicated on May 30, 1870, at the old public square at the northeast corner of Limestone and Columbia streets, 3,000 citizens gathered for the occasion. Eleven days earlier others had watched as William McIntire and Sons labored to move the thirty-ton monument of antique bronze from the railroad depot to the site.

The five years between the end of the war and the dedication of the monument were momentous ones. Congress passed the Reconstruction Act to restore the Union. Congressman Samuel Shellabarger defined the middle ground between the radical Republicans of Thaddeus Stevens and the Democrats. His crucial amendment, which disenfranchised the Confederate leadership, ended the deadlock and Congress passed legislation governing the return of the Southern states.

Springfielders, however, were paying only partial attention to affairs in Washington. Things at home were too lively. One veteran who had gone to Indiana after the war returned seven years later and did not know where he was when he got off the train. "I looked off south and the town was all built up where before the war it had been largely swamp. I went north on Limestone Street and could recognize no landmarks. . .so great had been the change in a few years."

The demand for storerooms and dwellings was overwhelming. The town's population in 1860 was 7,002, by 1870 it had reached 12,652, and by 1880 it surpassed 20,000. From then on the population of the city exceeded that of the rest of the county. Rents advanced, the value of real estate appreciated rapidly, and building went on in all directions. In 1868 alone 250 new buildings were erected.

In 1869 local builder Alfred Raffensperger promoted the town's first great real estate development. He laid out East Springfield and took the first full-page advertisement ever seen in local newspapers to promote the sale. Residents considered it an extravagant show. On the day of the sale, he ran coaches all day long from town to his development. At the site he had a brass band, and velocipede riders from all over the state participated in stunts and races. The sale was a tremendous success.

New construction downtown also attracted attention. A grand new hotel, the Lagonda House, was built on the corner of High and Limestone streets by a number of local businessmen who saw the need for a first-class hotel. The five-story, 140-room hotel opened on September 30, 1869.

The moving force behind the Lagonda House was John W. Bookwalter. Bookwalter came to Springfield before the war and worked with successful inventor and industrialist James Leffel. Later he married Leffel's daughter and participated in the management of the James Leffel Company for half a century. He and Benjamin Warder, carrying on the Warder family's tradition of concern for culture, were the most prominent art collectors and art

Opposite
Champion Machine Company workers posed in front of their factory around 1880. The enterprise was formed in 1867 to fill the great demand for Champion reapers in the Southern and Western states and territories. CCHS

patrons in the city, and the Lagonda House reflected Bookwalter's taste. Bookwalter was not only a successful industrialist and art collector, he was also a candidate for governor in 1882. He was a world traveler and the author of several books, including one on the American West and one on Siberia. Although he did not attend college himself, he endowed a chair of philosophy at Wittenberg.

Downtown, businessman Andrew C. Black opened Black's Opera House, which seated 1,000. The first performance was *The Drummer Boy of Shiloh* on February 8, 1869. The opera house was a five-story building with storerooms on the first floor, the theater on the second,

Left
Union Hall, pictured circa 1929 on South Fountain Avenue, was built in 1874. From 1877 to 1890 it housed the local library. CCHS

Below
The East County Building was one of 250 new structures erected in Springfield during 1869. It provided offices for the county treasurer, auditor, recorder, commissioners, and board of agriculture. This photograph was taken circa 1890, when the building housed the Probate Court. CCHS

and offices on the upper three floors. Invitations were extended to state associations and fraternal groups to hold meetings in the town and take advantage of these new facilities.

Another area of progress was banking. With the passage of the National Banking Act during the Civil War, local banking opportunities expanded rapidly. In 1864 the Springfield branch of the Ohio State Bank was incorporated as the First National Bank by Asa S. Bushnell, a young local businessman (and twenty years later the governor of Ohio); Oscar T. Martin; Richard H. Rodgers; and John S. Crowell. The Mad River branch was incorporated as the Mad River National Bank in 1865.

In the same year private bankers William and Gustavus Foos, nephews of pioneer settler Griffith Foos, incorporated as the Second National Bank. During 1870 the Commercial Bank was opened, and three years later incorporated as the Lagonda National Bank with J. Warren Keifer as president. Keifer was notable as a Civil War general, attorney, member of Congress, and later Speaker of the United States House of Representatives. In 1881 industrialists Phineas P. Mast and John Foos, yet another nephew of Griffith Foos, incorporated the Springfield National Bank.

Above
The five-story, 140-room Lagonada House was built on the corner of High and Limestone streets by a coalition of Springfield businessmen who saw a need for a first-rate hotel. It opened for business on September 30, 1869. CCHS

Right
One of Springfield's main thoroughfares is seen as it appeared in 1889, with horse and carriage tracks, recently installed telephone lines, and muddy streets. This busy intersection of horse-and-buggy days, looking north on Limestone Street at High Street, is still one of Springfield's main arteries. Today the core-renewal block and new Credit Life building would be seen at the left and, lining the streets on the right, the modern buildings of the Security National Bank and the Merchant & Mechanics Savings and Loan. CCHS

Left
Black's Opera House, at the corner of Main Street and Fountain Avenue, was built in 1868 at a cost of $100,000. The 1,000-seat auditorium was located on the second floor, and the first floor was occupied by storerooms. CCHS

Opposite, top
The First National Bank was incorporated in 1864 by Asa S. Bushnell, Oscar T. Martin, Richard H. Rodgers, and J.S. Crowell. This picture of the bank was published in 1875. Courtesy, Warder Memorial Library

Opposite, bottom left
Ross Mitchell, Springfield industrialist and philanthropist, was associated in the Champion interests. He was also the owner of Black's Opera House and staged productions in it until it was destroyed by fire in 1903. Mitchell spearheaded the drive to build Recitation Hall, the second building on the Wittenberg campus. Along with John M. Thomas, he provided Springfield with a hospital in 1890. Mitchell was photographed circa 1875. CCHS

Opposite, bottom right
J. Warren Keifer, lawyer, soldier, statesman, author, and civic leader, worked on the family farm while he studied law as a youth. His long and active career included fourteen years in Congress and the role of Speaker of the House from 1881 to 1883. Keifer was a major general in the Civil War and returned again to active service during the Spanish-American War. CCHS

These were the focal points for the financing of local businesses. Three building and loan associations developed to help local citizens accumulate savings and finance home purchases: the Springfield Savings Society in 1874, the Springfield Building and Loan Association in 1884, and the Merchants and Mechanics Savings and Loan Association in 1892.

William and Gustavus Foos were representative of the new industrialists in the years following the Civil War. The Foos brothers arrived the year before the war and became involved in mercantile and real estate dealings. They bought and developed a tract of land on east High Street, which became the best residential section of the city. With the proceeds they entered the banking business.

In 1866 William Foos joined the James Leffel Company, where he remained until 1876. After that he devoted his energies to real-estate development in Ohio and Illinois. Gustavus entered the wool business and made great profits. In the depression of 1873 he lost most of his fortune, but he recouped his losses making kitchen clothes wringers and special grinding and pulverizing machinery. He was joined in business by his sons Robert and William, and their Foos Manufacturing Company became well-known through the turn of the coming century.

Phineas P. Mast was another entrepreneur whose businesses flourished in the years following the Civil War. His P.P. Mast Company manufactured Buckeye grain drills, seeders and sowers, cultivators, and cider mills. He invested in other businesses, helping local entrepreneurs to get a start. Later he joined forces with the Foos interests and

formed the Mast, Foos Company, which made Buckeye lawnmowers, force pumps, wind engines, and iron fencing. The genial Mast served two years as mayor of Springfield and was a staunch advocate of civic responsibility.

The success story of the era, however, was that of William Whitely and the Champion reaper. Whitely and his partner Jerome Fassler, a mechanic of infinite skill, possessed great mechanical ability but little capital. They began manufacturing their reaper with their own hands. During 1856, their first year, they made and sold twenty reapers. The flamboyant Whitely entered his machine in state and county fairs in competition with rivals and won enough prizes to dub his machine the *Champion* reaper. To show its working ease he unhitched the horses and pulled it himself. In one famous advertisement of the era, Whitely even showed the Champion reaper being pulled by a chicken!

In 1857 Whitely and Fassler received an influx of capital from Oliver S. Kelly. Kelly was a Springfield resident who had gone to California in 1852, where he prospered building houses for the growing population in that state. He returned to Springfield in 1856 and used his savings to enter the wholesale grocery business. In 1857 he purchased an interest in the Whitely and Fassler Company, which he held until 1881.

The Civil War provided increased profits for the Whitely company, and a noticeable expansion. "It didn't amount to a very great deal until about the time of the war," observed one resident. The increased demand for the farm machinery was so great that Whitely could not

keep up with it. In 1867 he contracted with Warder, Mitchell and Company to make reapers, and in the same year a new company, the Champion Machine Company, was formed to manufacture the machine for Southern and Western states and territories.

These three companies—Whitely, Fassler, and Kelly; Warder, Mitchell and Company; and the Champion Machine Company—became known as the Champion interests, and their prosperity gave Springfield its nickname, "The Champion City." In 1874 the companies organized the Champion Malleable Iron Company, which bought out Springfield Malleable Iron. The new company produced 3,000 tons of quality iron annually to supply the Champion interests. In the same year the companies organized the Champion Bar and Knife Company to make cutter bars, guards, knives, sickles, and sections.

In 1875 the three companies acquired a railroad line to the coal fields of Southern Ohio. The Ohio Southern Railroad ran from Springfield to South Charleston, Jeffersonville, Washington Court House, Waverly, and Jackson. The capital stock was owned by members of the Champion interests, and the line brought coal, charcoal, and mill iron to the five Champion companies.

The Champion reaper became Springfield's major product. At one time the value of reapers equaled the value of all other products, and Springfield became the leading manufacturer of farm machinery in the world. The Depression of 1873 to 1877, which affected so many so harshly, barely touched Springfield because of the Champion's worldwide sales. Springfield newspapers noted that banks were cashing all checks, factories were running full speed and working overtime, and business was prospering. On April 24, 1877, four trains of seventy-two cars left Springfield carrying 1,618 Champion machines to market, the largest consignment of reapers and mowers the world had ever seen.

In 1881 Kelly withdrew from the Whitely and Fassler Company. Worried about Whitely's flamboyant style, he preferred to operate on his own. He continued to manufacture the Champion reaper and later manufactured threshing machines, engines, separators, rollers, piano plates, and a host of other products. He was connected in banking interests with the Warders and built the Arcade Hotel on Fountain Square.

Kelly was also prominent in public life, serving six years on the city council and as a waterworks trustee. Later he served as mayor and contributed to the development and beautification of the downtown area. In 1877 Mill Run was closed over with brick and stone arches from the spot where the Whitely, Fassler, and Kelly plant was located to Center Street. Changing this stream to an underground sewer prepared the way for downtown development. During Kelly's term as mayor in 1887, the new

City Building was completed. When the esplanade was laid out between the Arcade Hotel and the new City Building, it was graced with a beautiful fountain, a gift to the city from Mayor Kelly. Market Street was renamed Fountain Avenue.

Another entrepreneur and inventor associated with the booming agricultural implements business was William Bayley, who came to the city after the war to "find an opportunity" and was offered a job by Whitely. He worked at Whitely's plant until 1882, when he launched his own company doing experimental iron work and making steel windows for office buildings.

Springfield's prosperity in the midst of general economic trouble attracted attention and also some new opportunities for growth, but the economic climate also stiffened the competition for those opportunities. One tough competition was for the location of The Ohio State University. During the Civil War, Congress passed the Land Grant College Act, giving each state a grant of lands for a college of agriculture and mechanical arts. It was not until after the war, however, that Ohio resolved the political issues involved in accepting its grant. Fear of a new, well-financed institution with a practical curriculum galvanized existing colleges into action. Ohio and Miami universities, together with private and church-related institutions, met in Springfield in 1867 to organize The Ohio College Association to uphold classical college standards. President Sprecher of Wittenberg was the group's first president.

In 1870 the legislature restricted the location of the new college to a "centrally located industrial city," effectively limiting the choice to Springfield or Columbus. In September Springfield residents voted for a bond issue to entice the Board of the Ohio Agricultural and Mechanical College to pick Springfield. The vote was 1,462 in favor to 37 against. The board visited Springfield to consider two sites—the Cooper farm north of town and the Benjamin Warder farm east of town. The Springfield Street Railway Company offered to build a line from the center of town to the Warder farm if that site was selected.

Later in the month, after twenty-six ballots, the board voted for Columbus over Springfield. Columbus interests were so divided, however, that in October the board asked Springfield to renew its offer. Success for Springfield seemed imminent, but on October 13, with Governor Rutherford B. Hayes lobbying for Columbus, the board reaffirmed its earlier decision.

Springfield's case had been presented by industrialists John H. Thomas, John Ludlow, George Spence, Benjamin Warder, and William Whitely. Local civic leaders had agreed to add another $50,000 to the offer. Major railroads serving the area promised to add to the subscrip-

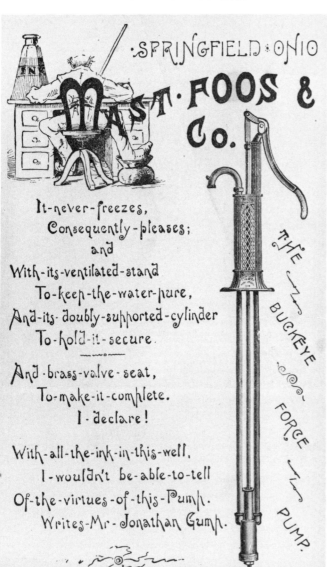

Above
Springfield's industry prospered after the Civil War. The Springfield Machine Tool Company factory is pictured as it appeared circa 1890 in this drawing by Horace Wheeler. CCHS

Left
The Buckeye force pump was one of several handy items manufactured by the Mast, Foos Company. According to this ad of the era, "it never freezes" and "consequently pleases."

Below
Oliver S. Kelly brought California gold to Springfield and became one of the city's leading entrepreneurs. He also served on the city council and later became Mayor of Springfield. Courtesy, Warder Memorial Library

43

tion. All were to no avail. The fairness of the decision was questioned by some Springfielders, who noted that two members of the board, John Buchtel and Cornelius Aultman of Akron, manufactured the Buckeye mower and reaper in competition with Whitely's Champion reaper. Given Whitely's flourish for advertising and promotion, there was no doubt in the minds of his competitors that he would use the university to their disadvantage.

The rivalry of the two interests played into the hands of those who sought to centralize state affairs in Columbus. Columbus soon became the location for the hospital for the insane, the state penitentiary, and the state fair, as well as the new university. The loss of the university rankled Springfielders, and they charged that the major losers were farmers, for the Agricultural and Mechanical College soon changed its name to The Ohio State University and adopted a curriculum like that of existing colleges and universities. Agricultural education was not to be the school's major emphasis.

There were two long-term results for the city of Springfield. The first was strained relations between the town's industrialists and Wittenberg College. The second was the birth of *Farm and Fireside* magazine, forerunner of one of the city's most famous enterprises.

The strained relations with Wittenberg were unfortunate. When the town's leaders failed to win the agricultural college, they decided to make Wittenberg into one. Every industrial town in Ohio wanted a vocationally oriented school, and industrialists could not understand the reluctance of the older colleges. The group in Springfield offered to add $50,000 to Wittenberg's endowment if they would be permitted to pick the occupants of three chairs—agriculture, mechanical arts, and political economy. The Wittenberg Board refused to make such a drastic change in its classical curriculum or to give outsiders such power over faculty selection, and tensions rose. When Wittenberg sought other financial support in the community, the effort failed, and the board considered moving the school to Mansfield or Lima.

In the resolution of the conflict, Dr. John B. Helwig resigned as president on May 1, 1882, to be replaced by Samuel Ort, another faculty member. Local businessman Ross Mitchell chaired a new fund drive and sufficient gifts were pledged to build Recitation Hall. The pledges brought Wittenberg's facilities up to a more competitive level, but without a change in its basic educational philosophy. Later John W. Bookwalter indicated approval for that cause by his gift to endow a chair of philosophy.

The appearance of *Farm and Fireside* magazine had a different result. P.P. Mast began publishing a trade magazine to promote the products of his firm and related Champion interests. He got the idea from John W. Bookwalter, who published the *Leffel Mechanical News* to promote the products and concepts of the James Leffel Company, and from John S. Crowell, publisher of the Louisville-based *Home and Farm*. Mast hired Crowell to start the Springfield publication. *Farm and Fireside* became more popular than Mast had envisioned. The firm of Mast, Crowell, and Kirkpatrick then hired Charles E. Thorne, former manager of the experimental farm at Ohio State, as editor. He used *Farm and Fireside* to attack Ohio State for not meeting the needs of Ohio farmers. The battle was a long one, but after several years the program at the school was modified to make agricultural field work and experimentation more important. In the process *Farm and Fireside*'s circulation passed 200,000, and the magazine reached more than one million readers, champion of the interests of farmers across the Midwest.

In 1881 the publications were moved into their own building at the corner of Wittenberg Avenue and High Street. In 1883 the firm acquired the children's magazine *Home Companion*, which became *Woman's Home Companion*, another successful magazine with a wide circulation. Additions were made to the structure in 1891 and again in 1903. In 1906 John Crowell sold the company, of which he had become sole owner at the turn of the century, to Joseph Knapp of New York City. Knapp moved

Above
Springfield's City Building, facing Fountain Square, was nearing completion in this 1889 photograph. The City Market was housed on the block-long first floor, and municipal offices and police headquarters were on the upper floors. From the Paul Ballentine Collection

Above
Not all Clark County factories compared with the Champion interests in size. This small buggy-and-carriage maker was flourishing in nearby Enon in 1869. CCHS

Farm and Fireside, *started by Phineas P. Mast to promote the products of his firm, moved into its own building at Wittenberg Avenue and High Street in 1881. The firm of Mast, Crowell, and Kirkpatrick grew into Crowell-Collier Publishing Company and the building grew with it to cover a full city block. CCHS*

the central and editorial offices to New York, but continued to expand the plant in Springfield. The company acquired the *American* magazine in 1915 and *Collier's* in 1919 and became one of the nation's leading magazine-publishing enterprises.

Despite the successful economic expansion, the years following the Civil War were not without some problems. For one thing, the prosperity of the war and postwar eras left Springfield and other communities with serious alcohol problems. The free-flowing spirits and excess purchasing power made saloon-keeping a prosperous enterprise indeed. With the saloons came gambling, fighting, and prostitution. These were major problems for the nation, but seemed worse in industrial towns like Springfield.

Not long after the war Eliza Stewart, a Springfield housewife, began agitating for temperance. She engaged the Ladies Aid Society to assist and later enlisted the clergy. By 1872 "Mother" Stewart was emboldened to hold a public temperance meeting and to address it herself, rath-

er than ask a man sympathetic to the cause to do it for her. She called it the first step in a crusade. Groups of Mother Stewart's ladies picketed barrooms and saloons and created a growing public concern about the excesses of the liquor traffic.

In 1870 the Ohio constitution was amended to allow regulation and licensing of the liquor traffic. A series of bills passed the legislature. One made tavern keepers and liquor sellers liable for the effects of their businesses, and Mother Stewart encouraged the wives of drunkards to bring charges against tavern keepers and liquor dealers for selling to their husbands when they were already

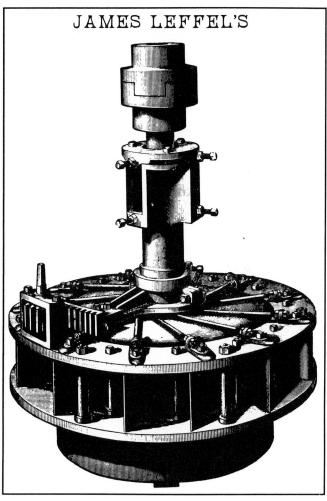

JAMES LEFFEL'S

Above
Wittenberg College President John B. Helwig resigned in 1874 in order to resolve the conflict over Springfielders' attempts to change the school's classical curriculum to one emphasizing vocational and agricultural education. In 1889 Helwig ran for governor on the prohibition ticket. From the Wittenberg University Archives

Top, right
James Leffel's tinkering developed into an industry of building water wheels. In the James Leffel & Company catalog of 1888, Leffel stated, "we are pleased to say ... that our wheel is now in use in every civilized country on the globe." Pictured is the improved double-turbine water wheel, which was the heart of the successful system. From the Paul Ballentine Collection

drunk and knowingly permitting them to spend more than they could afford, thus depriving their families of needed food and clothing. In one case she appeared in court as an adviser to a wife and made the closing remarks for the prosecution. The defense attorney was outraged and charged that Mother Stewart should be home attending to her duties. Yet Mother Stewart persevered and became a nationally known leader in the Women's Christian Temperance Union.

In 1874 and again in 1877 statewide conventions of the crusaders were held in Springfield. Some were shocked when the convention declared that if women were to destroy the curse of alcohol they would first have to acquire the right to vote. It was a revolutionary and disconcerting

idea for many. Others were startled when in 1874 Wittenberg opened its doors to women and became a coeducational college.

The temperance crusade continued through the 1880s. In 1889 the Reverend John B. Helwig, pastor of First Lutheran Church and the former president of Wittenberg, ran for governor on the prohibition ticket. He delivered sixty-five speeches in thirty-two counties and pulled over 24,000 votes.

Racial tensions presented another set of concerns for the town. Following the war black migration to the area encountered new white migration from the Appalachian South. While during the war there was strong support for enfranchising blacks, support decreased with each passing year. By 1870 Clark County's black population had reached 2,056, mostly in the city, and Springfield's black population approached nearly fifteen percent. In 1872 black citizens met in Asbury Chapel on South Center Street, an area of black settlement, to draw up petitions asking the school board to open schools to black children. The resolutions called attention to the rights of all

Recitation Hall, the second building constructed on the Wittenberg College campus, was built from 1883 to 1884 with funds pledged by the people of Springfield. From the Wittenberg University Archives

Bicycling clubs were popular among the town's young men. This particular group of enthusiasts posed on the steps of Wittenberg's Recitation Hall circa 1885. CCHS

The Arcade Hotel, built by Oliver S. Kelly, anchored the south end of the Arcade Building. In this circa 1889 photograph the fountain on the esplanade, for which Fountain Square was named, was under construction (left). From the Paul Ballentine Collection

citizens under the Fifteenth Amendment and the Civil Rights Bill. Several white citizens also signed the petition, including General J. Warren Keifer and Oscar T. Martin, an attorney.

The school board denied the petition and made plans for a separate school for black children. Black parents arrived at a number of schools to enroll their children but were turned away. Since there was no black high school, the parents of Broadwell Chinn petitioned that he be admitted to the white school. He was a bright, well-prepared young man, but he was denied admission. The principal and some of the teachers later tutored him in off hours, over the objections of white students.

When Broadwell Chinn finished high school he applied to Wittenberg. The faculty decided that they had no authority to admit him and put the matter to a vote of the students, who turned him down. President Helwig took the matter to the board of directors, who reversed the students' decision and reproved the faculty. There was no race barrier at Wittenberg, the board insisted, consistent with the abolitionist views of the school's founders. Chinn later studied law in Springfield and was elected a member of the Clark County Bar Association.

The Chinn story illustrates the rise of segregation and Jim Crow attitudes in the decades following the war. This was troubling for many like General Keifer and Congressman Samuel Shellabarger. Broadwell Chinn proved that there was a chance for some blacks to get ahead, but the chance was limited.

Increasing industrial expansion in the 1880s brought

with it labor unrest. Whitely's agricultural machinery plant, Springfield's leader in this industrial expansion, was also the focus of labor troubles.

In 1881 William Whitely was convinced that he could corner an ever-growing share of the market and wanted to build a larger factory. When his partners Kelly and Fassler disagreed with his plans, Whitely bought them out. Whitely then bought a large tract of land on East Street and built the massive East Street Shops, the second-largest factory in the world, second only to the Krupp Works in Germany. Whitely's new plant employed 2,000 workers. Before long 1,000 of these workers were affiliated with the Knights of Labor.

Prior to the Civil War there were no labor unions in Clark County. The first, the Iron Molders, was organized in 1864 with twenty-two charter members, many of whom later became private entrepreneurs. The Iron Molders paid sick and unemployment benefits and had an agreement with employers that all disputes were to be heard by a joint committee. The second union, the Typographical Union, was established in 1868. The typographers called a strike in 1886, but it was brief and the matter was settled by arbitration. No other unions were organized until 1883 when the Locomotive Engineers and the Knights of Labor appeared. Seventeen unions were organized in the 1880s, reflecting the rapid industrial growth.

The Mad River Assembly of the Knights was organized in 1883. During the recession of 1883 to 1886, eleven more assemblies were organized, and in the latter year Springfield was designated a district assembly. The Knights were growing, and a test of strength with the city's largest employer was inevitable. The Knights had caused trouble in a number of places, and Whitely feared they would cause trouble in Springfield. He considered labor agitation a violation of his property rights. He issued orders for the discharge of men who would not sign an ironclad agreement

Above
Workers like these employees of the O.S. Kelly Company, photographed in 1900, were fundamentally conservative, but willing to listen to "talk of union." This greatly distressed some employers, who would rather they did not. CCHS

Right
The Springfield Metallic Casket Company, photographed in 1889, was one of the city's fastest growing industries. In 1932 its workers staged a sit-down strike and took over the plant. CCHS

not to join a union. He had a large sign placed across the front of his shop declaring that "free and independent workmen only" would be employed.

Springfield was tense for weeks. Whitely would allow no man to work who had not renounced the Knights. The men considered themselves "locked out" and asked the national union to boycott Whitely's machines. The effect of the boycott was never known because in June 1887 Whitely's empire collapsed. The Springfield *Daily Gazette* designated Friday, June 17, Blue Friday, the greatest business disaster in the history of Springfield. The Fidelity National Bank of Cincinnati failed because of futures speculation by a man with whom Whitely had coal and iron dealings. The two had "signed each other's paper" guaranteeing payment if either failed to make good. Whitely, unable to make good on Harper's debts, saw his own interests collapse.

Whitely, who held 125 patents and was considered one of the area's greatest inventors, became known as the man who "made and broke Springfield." His collapse, however, did not destroy the Champion interests. The separate companies like Warder, Mitchell, and Glessner survived and continued to manufacture Champion products. In 1879 Ross Mitchell retired from the company, but the

other two partners incorporated with banker and businessman Asa S. Bushnell as Warder, Bushnell, and Glessner. They continued in operation until 1902, then merged with four other companies in the International Harvester Company.

Whitely turned his assets over to an assignee, banker Joseph Warren Keifer, but because of conflicts Keifer resigned. Attorney George H. Frey succeeded him. The East Street Shops, built in 1881 at a cost of $1.2 million, were sold at auction for $200,000. The building stood idle for some time, and 2,000 Springfielders were out of work. It was the first serious economic setback in the town's eighty-year history.

Mayor Oliver Kelly asked local businessmen to deal with the crisis. He organized the Board of Trade, which

Above
Picnicking was a pleasant and acceptable social activity for young people in the Gay Nineties. This Christian Endeavor group enjoyed an outing in Clifton in 1892. CCHS

Below
The lovely home of Jacob Sietz, pictured about 1880, was situated at the southwest corner of North Limestone and North streets. The house and the adjoining land were later owned by C.F. McGilvrary, general manager of Robbins and Myers and Mayor of Springfield for a term. When McGilvrary died in 1922 his widow donated the property to the Young Men's Christian Association. Upon her death in 1935 the YMCA received a bequest of $300,000 for a new building, which was built on the site and completed in 1939. Today this is the location of Springfield's McGilvrary YMCA. CCHS

Above
Springfield's Central High School building, pictured in 1889, was erected in 1875 on the southwest corner of West High Street and Wittenberg Avenue, across from what became the Crowell-Collier building. In 1911 a new school, today Springfield South High School, was built on South Limestone Street. CCHS

This magnificent mansion at 838 East High Street was the home of Governor and Mrs. Asa S. Bushnell in 1896. Today the building is occupied by the Austin Richards and Raff Memorial Home. It is one of Springfield's best examples of Richardson Romanesque architecture. CCHS

later became the Springfield Area Chamber of Commerce. Attorney and banker Oscar T. Martin was elected president. Other leaders were Theo Troupe, S.J. Wilkerson, D. Thornton West, and J. Frank McGrew. They persuaded one of the partners of the Krell-French Piano Company of Cincinnati to purchase the north wing of the East Street Shops. In 1885 the Wickham Piano Plate Company started in Springfield, and that was an added inducement. Unfortunately the great East Street Shops were never again fully utilized.

Most workmen felt that Whitely misunderstood the intentions of the Knights and that local industrialists failed to understand their need to organize. Efforts continued. In 1890 the Springfield Trades and Labor Assembly was founded as an organization to bring unions together in confederation. The assembly promoted the celebration of Labor Day. In 1890 it scheduled the Grand Master Workman of the Knights of Labor, Terrence V. Powderly, to speak, and he addressed a large Labor Day gathering on the Esplanade. In 1891 the assembly heard Eugene V. Debs, head of the Socialist Party. Still later their speaker was Samuel Gompers of the American Federation of Labor.

Whitely's opposition to organized labor typified the views of area industrialists, but they were not without concern for their workers. They founded savings banks, home loan associations, and temperance societies for the benefit of their employees. Other aspects of local paternalism included personal charity in times of need, but a stern rebuke for drunkenness, swearing, waste, or inactivity.

Benevolent paternalism was also evidenced in support of the local library. From the 1830s Jeremiah Warder had supported the library and reading room as a place for workingmen to properly advance themselves. In 1868 the YMCA took over operation. In 1872 a new library was opened in Black's Opera House, and in 1877 it was moved to Union Hall. Finally, in 1890, the Warder Free Public Library building was dedicated.

The YMCA itself had been promoted as a redeeming activity, particularly for younger workmen. The organization encouraged Bible study, character development, and athletics both in the town and at the college. By the 1880s the YMCA was promoting basketball teams for most companies and among storekeepers, as well as at Wittenberg. Bicycling clubs, baseball teams, and track-and-field events were popular.

Through the efforts of Dr. John Rodgers, the YMCA had secured a tract of land 100 yards or so east of North Limestone Street, between Stanton Avenue and Cassilly Street. It extended east to the Old Mill Race where residents swam and boated. It was a popular place for college students and townsfolk alike to enjoy picnics, weekend

recreation, and athletic contests that pitted teams from various factories against one another. The fields included baseball diamonds, tennis courts, a running track, a football field, a small fieldhouse, and bleachers seating 250. Until Snyder Park was dedicated, it was the center for outdoor recreation and one of the best facilities in the state.

Other city amenities also grew. In 1871 P.P. Mast and George Spence provided horse- and mule-drawn streetcar service. They were premature, but by 1882 regular service was profitable. Springfield's first telephones were installed in the 1870s on the Dayton Exchange. By 1880 Springfield had its own company, and sixty-eight phones were installed. By 1883, 250 subscribers were listed in the directory. That same year the Springfield Electric Power Company began providing service to local customers. Springfield had electricity before many other towns. The first electric plant in the United States had opened in New York City in 1882, and Springfield's plant came a year later, the enterprise of O.S. Kelly. The first electric lights were installed at Kinane's Department Store, now the Blocks/Wrens store. Street lights soon followed downtown, and visitors came from miles around to see them. By 1887 electric streetcars made Springfield "The City of Tomorrow."

Public facilities were also improved. In 1881 the new county courthouse opened. In 1890 the new City Building opened at Fountain Square. The city hospital, a gift from wealthy industrialists Ross Mitchell and John H. Thomas, opened on East Main Street.

In 1895 John and David L. Snyder, two farmers living west of town, donated the 217 acres adjoining Mad River and Buck Creek for a city park. In 1898 the surviving brother bequeathed $200,000 to endow the park's upkeep.

Much had changed since the war, and the change was apparent in the shift from Shellabarger to Keifer and Bushnell as the state's leading Republicans. Samuel Shellabarger had been the friend of Jeremiah Warder and other early promoters of the city. His political career evolved with the young Republican party and reflected

Above
The new City Hospital, a gift of Ross Mitchell and John M. Thomas, opened on East Main Street in 1890. CCHS

Left
Pictured in 1905 are the Power Street carbarns and the streetcars of the Springfield Railway Company. CCHS

the free-trade beliefs of the Champion interests. In 1869 President Grant named him Minister to Portugal as a reward for his services. In 1870 he returned in order to prevent J. Warren Keifer from getting the GOP nomination for Congress. He then defeated Democrat Hugh J. Jewett, counsel for the Pennsylvania Railroad, in the fall election.

Following that term, Shellabarger retired from Congress. He was named by Grant to serve on the nation's first Civil Service Commission, but after a year he resigned to enter private law practice in Washington, D.C. He was defense attorney in virtually every major case in Washington for fifteen years: the Star Route mail frauds, the Sugar Trust bribery cases, and the trial of the district's Boss Shepherd. In 1876 when the outcome of the presidential election was in doubt between Hayes and Tilden, Hayes asked Shellabarger to be his personal attorney and protect his interests and reputation as the parties maneuvered to settle the dispute. Shellabarger appeared periodically in Springfield and was saluted by the town's black citizens for his role in emancipation and Negro suffrage.

In 1877 Springfield's J. Warren Keifer was elected to Congress, representing the new forces in the Republican party. The new industrialists were advocates of a high tariff and other policies sympathetic to business. Keifer served in the Congress from 1877 to 1885 and was Speaker of the House from 1881 to 1883. He served again in the Congress from 1906 to 1911. He represented the bustling, industrial giant that Springfield had become.

Asa S. Bushnell was the leading Republican at home. Successful in business as president of Warder, Bushnell, and Glessner, president of the Springfield Gas Company, and president of the First National Bank, his record as a politician was equally impressive. In 1885 he became chairman of the Republican State Executive Committee. In 1886 he was named Quartermaster General of Ohio. He was proposed as a candidate for governor twice before accepting the nomination in 1895, and he was twice elected.

Local industrial leaders remained staunchly Republican and actively campaigned among their workmen. In the 1896 election, for instance, the Mast, Crowell, and Kirkpatrick Company posted a picture of William McKinley in every one of the 100 windows in their four-story building.

As the nineteenth century ended Springfield had achieved great growth and had survived some serious problems. The city was prosperous, proud, and confident of its future. When it called itself "The Champion City," it had more in mind than reapers—it had in mind the spirit of a champion community.

Successful Springfield businessman Asa S. Bushnell was twice elected governor of Ohio. Governor Bushnell is pictured in his 1896 inaugural photograph. CCHS

Ellen Ludlow Bushnell, wife of Springfield industrialist and Ohio governor Asa S. Bushnell, is pictured in her 1896 inaugural gown. CCHS

5 The Gay Nineties and a Golden Age

The decade of the 1890s was one of nationwide economic depression. Unemployment was so harsh that a class of permanently poor became increasingly evident. It was also a period of emerging affluence, however, and its visibility gave the era its nickname, the Gay Nineties.

Springfield reflected this growing national dichotomy, yet there seemed to be more gaiety than hardship. When the town fathers took firm action on area problems, they ushered in a golden age that lasted through World War I and the Roaring Twenties. The city and county emerged prosperous and self-contained, with rich culture and strong local leadership. The area's prosperity supported a good quality of life. Citizens saw their lives as fulfilled within the county borders. While reaping the benefits of the area, citizens also felt a responsibility to contribute to its welfare. They became hometown boosters.

Springfield took the depression of 1893 to 1897 in stride, as it had the previous one, because the continuous progress of industry and trade overwhelmed the problems. The city's upward momentum was simply too great. Its population and industry outpaced decline. The average Springfielder shared the prosperity when Cyrus B. Kissell, who started in the real estate business in 1884, developed ways to make home owning easier. By 1894 the C.B. Kissell Company was Springfield's most prominent real estate and loan agent. Many regarded Kissell as the man who got them their home. One of his devices was the double house, in which the owner lived on one side while renting the other, and the rent carried the mortgage. Springfield became a community with more double houses than any town in America.

The town took the Spanish-American War in stride, too. A number of Ohio National Guard companies were called up, and area residents were included. General J. Warren Keifer reentered the army for service in this war. Local residents debated the issues of America's debut as an imperial power, but the issues were not as important locally as the issues of the Civil War had been.

In August 1901 Springfield celebrated the centennial of its founding. An entire week of festivities was devoted to the celebration. A gala parade kicked off activities. Edgar N. Lupfer, a local leather goods manufacturer, was chief marshal and led a long line of bands, floats, and marching organizations to the fairgrounds on Pleasant Street. Presentations were made throughout the week. Some recognized the city's past, others saluted its present and future. One traced the town's commercial, political, and industrial history, another reminisced about the earliest settlers. Still others were dedicated to the professions—law, medicine, and military. Tribute was paid to the town's printing and publishing history, as well as its agriculture and labor, and salutations were extended to the roles of women and education.

The town was proud of its past and supremely confident of its future. The citizens saw themselves and their town as one of America's greatest success stories.

The town had also picked up a new name for itself— The Home City. In 1897 the Ohio Masonic Home opened in Springfield. In 1898 the Ohio Odd Fellows Home was dedicated. At the turn of the century the Knights of Pythias opened a home on McCreight Avenue, and Mrs. Charlotte S. Clark established a home for women on

Opposite
General J. Warren Keifer (seated, right) was called to service during the Spanish-American War. In this 1898 photograph Keifer meets with President McKinley (seated, left center) and (from left, standing) Major Generals Wheeler, Lawton, and Shafter. CCHS

Horace C. Keifer (pictured) of the Third Ohio Volunteer Engineers was an aide-de-camp for his father General J. Warren Keifer during the Spanish-American War in 1898. CCHS

North Limestone Street in memory of her son. Not long after the town's centennial, Ohio Lutherans founded the Oesterlen Home for Children on Lagonda Avenue. Springfield became Ohio's home city because it was connected to every part of Ohio by railroads and interurban lines. Fifty-four passenger trains arrived in Springfield daily, and the streetcar ran to Dayton, Urbana, Bellefontaine, Columbus, Xenia, and Troy. Anyone could visit relatives with ease.

Springfield also became known as a center of musical culture. Black's Opera House and the Grand Opera House made Springfield a stop for touring groups. In 1890 the famous Eduard Strauss and his magnificent fifty-piece Vienna orchestra toured America, and Springfield was included on the itinerary! In the same year famed Civil War bandmaster Patrick Sarsfield Gilmore brought his band to Springfield. Later, Vladamir de Pachman, a world-renowned performer of the music of Chopin, played Springfield. In 1916 the town proudly presented a five-

program concert series that included violinist Fritz Kreisler and the Philadelphia Symphony Orchestra.

The Wittenberg College Glee Club and Orchestra, under the leadership of Dr. Robert H. Hiller, added another dimension to Springfield's musical culture and reputation. The musical ensemble toured Cleveland, Akron, Columbus, Fort Wayne, Indianapolis, and Chicago. Several industries and fraternal groups maintained bands, and all of the churches had choirs and quartets. The Springfield Choral Society organized an annual spring music festival.

In 1904 Gus Sun opened a vaudeville theater, beginning his long career in Springfield as a theater operator and booking agent. In 1906 the Fairbanks Theater opened with a performance of *Ben Hur.* The theater was part of Springfield's first skyscraper, the eight-story First National Bank Building. Harry Kissell put together the real estate and financial package for it. In 1908 Philip Chakeres opened his first movie theater, the Princess. By 1916 the town boasted a legitimate theater with actual drama, a vaudeville theater, and eight movie houses. This essential element of the Gay Nineties, musical and theatrical entertainment, was well established in Springfield. The local hit parade included such tunes as "Bird in a Gilded Cage," "Hot Time in the Old Town," "After the Ball," and "When You Were Sweet Sixteen."

One aspect of the turn-of-the-century town was the *club.* There were a variety of men's clubs, including the prominent Lagonda Club, which was built in 1895 and is now in the historical register. Most typical were the lodges of the Masons, Odd Fellows, and Knights of Pythias. By 1900 there were nearly 100 different fraternal groups in Springfield with more than 11,000 members. Edwin S. Todd, a professional sociologist, noted that, "There are very few men in the city who do not belong to at least one of these organizations, and many belong to more than one." The Odd Fellows were the strongest, with the Masons and Knights of Pythias ranking second and third respectively. There were nine Masonic lodges for black men with 430 members, and five black Knights of Pythias lodges with 325 members. Another 250 black men belonged to various other groups.

The rest of the county was also full of lodges, with either the Knights of Pythias or the Junior Order of United American Mechanics in virtually every village and hamlet. The lodges provided social activities, amateur dramatics in fantastic costumes, and life and unemployment insurance. The orders also took care of a man's widow and orphans in the event of death and provided care for the elderly.

As men found support and enjoyment in lodges, women found them in women's clubs. Most women's groups still centered around church circles—the breeding ground for the woman's club—but the Civil War had broken the

Above
The Ohio Pythian Home was erected on East McCreight in 1900 and had accomodations for 250 men, women, and children. The eighty-six-acre site was purchased by Springfield members of the organization and others for $25,000 and donated for the purpose. From the Paul Ballentine Collection

Top
The Ohio Masonic Home opened west of Springfield on the National Road in 1897 and covered 154 acres. Originally it provided room for 250 men, women, and children. The generosity of Asa Bushnell and other Springfielders secured the location. From the Paul Ballentine Collection

Right
The Odd Fellows of Ohio selected Springfield as the location of their home for "widows and orphans and aged members of the order." The house was built on seventy-six acres of farmland and was dedicated in 1898. CCHS

Opposite
Music had an important place in the Springfield community by the end of the nineteenth century. Hawken's Cadet Band was well-known in the city and surrounding states. Pictured circa 1885 are (from left) band members E.K. Hawken, Frank Graham, Thomas P. Fetter, Charles Corti, Charles Deam, John Dogger, LaFevre, John Schafer, William Zubrod, and C. Spangenberger. CCHS

Right
Gus Sun opened a vaudeville theatre in Springfield on South Limestone Street in 1905 and became a leading impresario. His circuit bookings included such notables as Walter Winchell, Jack Dempsey, Will Rogers, Mae West, and the Marx Brothers. He later bought the Grand Opera House, had it razed, and in 1919 built the Regent Theatre on its site. CCHS

Below
Park Pavilion at Spring Grove (later Avalon) Park was a booming recreation spot for many years after the turn of the century. Its facilities included two small lakes and later a pavilion for dancing. Even though it enjoyed a sizable degree of popularity, no success in rebuilding the park was achieved after a devastating fire reduced the pavilion to ashes in the late 1920s. CCHS

The Pennsylvania Railroad Depot on South Fountain, built at the turn of the century, reflected the optimism of the city and helped service its share of Springfield's fifty-four daily passenger trains. From the Paul Ballentine Collection

barrier to wider organization. Women had worked in the interdenominational Soldiers Aid Society. Some women provided child-care services to working mothers. The female-dominated temperance societies of the 1870s led women to involvement with the Chautauqua movement. By the turn of the century, the women's club was common.

The Women's Benevolent Society operated an industrial school to teach female children of the poor to sew, set and wait a table, make beds, and cook. The school served nearly 200 girls in 1900. The Young Woman's Mission, founded in 1897, enlisted young women from more prosperous homes to alleviate distress among the sick poor. Another women's group was the Women's Christian Association, which grew out of the Deaconess Home. Its aims were similar to those of the YMCA, and it welcomed women of all ages.

Others women's groups included the Fortnightly Club, the Monday Afternoon Club, and the Tuesday Club. In 1896 these three clubs plus the Travelers Club organized the Springfield Women's Club, a focus for women's club and cultural activities.

Springfield was a flourishing community. It owed its prosperity to continuing industrial growth. By 1910 Springfield boasted a diversified industry of 141 different companies. Ten years later the number passed 200. At the city's centennial celebration William S. Thomas, a local industrialist and banker, had observed that growth would hinge on the same fundamentals that built the town: honest and competent men, cooperation between labor and management, quality products, drive, freedom from labor trouble, and ample capital from liberal banks. Thomas saw problems in the town's future but had no doubt of the ability of Springfielders to cope. One problem Thomas

observed was the national trend toward industry specialization. Springfield, he said, would have to diversify and increase the number of its enterprises to make up for businesses that would close or move. The other problem that Thomas saw was the expansion of world trade and its effect on Springfield's prosperity.

"The trade of this town is so extended now," Thomas said, "that wherever you go you will find Springfield represented, either by its products or its men." "Whatever happens all over this earth," he added, "has an influence here."

The 1900 census showed Springfield with a work force of 12,686 men and 2,809 women. Local observers were glad that Springfield women were willing to work in industries "where it has come to seem natural for women to be employed." It enabled Springfield to compete on a larger scale, but local businessmen were reluctant to "encourage too much the employment of our girls outside of homes where they can do such excellent, natural and beautiful service either as wives or mothers," according to Thomas.

The town boasted two breweries, however, the top beers—Red Head and Blue Head—were both produced by the Springfield Breweries, Ltd. They were promoted for use at home, at the club, and in the cafe. The beers were said to "bring good cheer when good fellows get together," and for the more traditional they were touted for their "muscle and health-giving power."

After the labor difficulties between William Whitely and the Knights of Labor, Springfield developed a stable labor market with relatively little unrest. Local leaders attributed this to several factors. First, Springfield had a relatively low cost of living. Second, local industrialists, encouraged by Cyrus B. Kissell, took the lead in developing savings banks and building and loan associations, making it possible for any man to own his home. Well-developed parks and amusement facilities and cultural opportunities added to the positive climate.

The diversity of local industry was also a factor. In addition Springfield workmen were fundamentally conservative, and not enthusiastic about increasingly radical tendencies in the labor movement.

Right
The eight-story First National Bank Building, Springfield's first skyscraper, was built in 1905 on the site of Black's Opera House, which was destroyed by fire. The new building also housed the Fairbanks Theater. CCHS

Below
During the early 1900s local businessmen were reluctant to encourage female employment. It was all right, however, for women to work "where it has come to seem natural for women to be employed." That apparently included the F.W. Woolworth Company store at 25-27 South Limestone Street. Mary Singer Bennett stands between the counters to the left, and Mrs. G. Frock is behind the candy counter to the right. Amid the Christmas decorations on display a large sign over the aisle guarantees "Nothing in this store over 10¢." CCHS

The Ohio Southern Railroad, "LIMA LINE." Makes Close Connections at All Junction Points.

SPECIAL RATES TO STUDENTS GOING TO AND FROM COLLEGE.

3 to 5 Hours Better Time than on Other Lines, from

SPRINGFIELD AND SOUTHERN OHIO.

TO

TOLEDO, DETROIT, CHICAGO, MICHIGAN POINTS AND THE——— NORTHWEST.

The Most Direct Route from

LIMA AND SPRINGFIELD,

TO

CHILLICOTHE, PARKERSBURG, WASHINGTON, D. C., BALTIMORE AND ALL POINTS IN THE VIRGINIAS AND——— SOUTHEAST.

20 BUYS A 1,000 MILE TICKET, GOOD OVER **71**

DOLLARS   ON SALE AT ALL STATIONS.   TRANSPORTATION LINES.

For Information Regarding Rates Route, Maps, etc., address

F. E. FISHER, Gen. Pass. Agt., SPRINGFIELD, O.

xx

The Springfield Employers Association announced the following objectives in 1915:

To secure for employers and employees freedom of contract in the matter of employment; to establish and maintain an employment bureau in the interest of both employer and employee; to oppose restriction of output, sympathetic strikes, and boycotts; to discountenance conditions which are not just or which will not allow a workman to earn a wage proportionate to his productive capacity; to prevent interference with those seeking work; to avert industrial disturbances; to harmonize differences between employers and employees so that justice may be done to both; to uphold the law.

The Association's objectives epitomized the views of Springfield industrialists who had risen from the ranks but firmly believed in their rights as owners. They saw nothing wrong with their opposition to organized labor so long as they were fair and listened to their employees. They knew their employees and their problems. They greeted their families by name when they met them on the street. Such men were greatly disturbed by the labor

The Ohio Southern Railroad was purchased by Henry Ford to supply coal to his Detroit operations. In this 1895 advertisement, special rates are offered to Wittenberg College students—1,000 miles of rail travel for $20. From the Wittenberg University Archives

unrest in the railroads, at Carnegie Steel, and elsewhere. Springfield industrialists sided with Ohio's Republican leader, Mark Hanna, who was enraged when George Pullman refused to arbitrate the great railroad strike of 1894. "A man who won't meet his men halfway," said Hanna, "is a Goddam fool." The Association was made less viable by centralization and absentee ownership, but Springfield employers held to their old ways.

Local legend has it that Henry Ford tried to buy a Springfield carriage factory as a site for automobile manufacturing, but was discouraged from doing so by employers who feared the effect of his higher pay scale. The pay scale in Springfield was sixteen to twenty dollars a week, while Ford reportedly planned to pay twenty-five dollars weekly. In reality Ford did not set the five-dollar-a-day wage until 1914, four years after his alleged offer to buy a Springfield plant.

64

Frank Lloyd Wright designed the Westcott House, built in 1905 at 1340 East High Street, for Burton J. Westcott, businessman and auto manufacturer. The two-story, stucco and concrete house has the characteristics of Wright's "prairie homes"—horizontal lines, low-pitched roof, broad eaves, wide verandas, stuccoed walls with wood trim, trellis work, and the elaborate use of shrubs with a spacious lawn. CCHS

While it is doubtful that Ford ever made an effort to locate in Springfield, Ford did have great interest in acquiring the Ohio Southern Railroad, which connected the town to the Southern Ohio coal fields. In the aftermath of the collapse of Whitely's enterprises, Ford bought the railroad from the Champion interests around 1910 and had it extended to his operations in Detroit, thus forming the Detroit, Toledo, and Ironton Railroad and gaining direct access to the coal fields. Once that was accomplished Ford's interest in Springfield dissipated. Later, from 1916 to 1926, an automobile was manufactured in Springfield. It was called the Westcott, and was built by Burton J. Westcott and his Westcott Motor Car Company.

Springfield participated in the centralization of American industry, as shown by two major developments on the local industrial scene. First, the local agricultural works became part of the Chicago-based International Harvester Company (IHC). With the help of J.P. Morgan's money, five of the nation's six largest reaper manufacturers merged into one giant corporation. Second, the Crowell-Collier Publishing Company moved its editorial offices (Crowell Publishing Company) to New York City, the nation's growing center for publishing and advertising.

Mechanical and printing operations remained in Springfield.

In both developments Springfield benefited from the trend toward expansion and centralization, but it also came to know absentee ownership. No longer would local workers at Crowell's or IHC meet their employers face-to-face, nor would the behavior of both parties be judged and influenced by local opinion.

Springfield also confronted a growing list of unfinished business that ultimately required a change in the city's form of government. By 1900 city population passed 38,000; a decade later the figure was 47,000; by 1920 the city bragged that it was the best 60,000-resident city in the western hemisphere! While the city nearly doubled in

Above
This four-door sedan was manufactured in Springfield in the early 1920s by the Westcott Motor Car Company and sold free on board to Springfield for $1,790. The Westcott boasted a six-cylinder continental motor; a Delco system of starting, lighting, and ignition; and all leather upholstery! CCHS

Top
Henry Ford's Model A was a worthy successor to the T, being the first car to have safety glass in its windshield as standard equipment. Although some may have been disappointed that Ford never established a plant in Springfield, he eventually purchased the Southern Ohio Railroad from the Champion interests and extended it to some of his other operations. CCHS

Above
Burton J. Westcott, Springfield businessman, civic leader, and manufacturer of Westcott motorcars, is pictured circa 1920. CCHS

size, the county population stayed even. Not including Springfield, the county population remained stable at 20,000 for several decades. Problems accompanying this rapid growth became more and more apparent.

Edwin S. Todd did a turn-of-the-century sociological study of Clark County—a dissertation at Columbia University. The Springfield native and Wittenberg graduate observed that his fellow townsmen were quick to feel but

slow to act on the problems of growth. They were not unlike people in other towns and cities; Springfield was in a state of transition. As one man told him, Springfield "has reached the full stature of a city but still retains many of the characteristics of village days."

Todd's list of unfinished business was extensive. People wanted better protection at railroad crossings, improved streets, street cleaning, a better sewer system, improved sanitary conditions, and improved water pressure. Until 1890, Todd observed, little thought had been given to the problems of street construction or cleaning. Between 1890 and 1900 all principal streets were paved, but the absence of street cleaning made them little better than before. Beginning in 1901 a system of cleaning was adopted and patterned after the plan developed in New York City.

Springfield still had garbage carted away by area farmers, and pickups were irregular and infrequent. The disposal of sewage was worse. Most dwellings still had "the old-fashioned private vault," and many were too shallow and poorly constructed. At the same time many residents used wells as a source of water, and the danger of septic tanks leaking into them was great. Sewage was carried off primarily by Buck Creek and Mill Run, and in the summer when the water flow was slow the streams' appearance and odor were offensive and a menace to public health.

Todd pointed to crime and law enforcement as another needs-work area for Springfield. He said that there was a lax administration of ordinances regulating saloons and gambling houses. Todd cited general opinion that the city existed for the good of the party spoilsman, and the electorate was unable to get reform. The result was a wide-open town. Saloons were open every day and night, gambling was rampant and unrestrained, and prostitution was a booming business. One of the worst areas was the Levee (or the Jungles) south of High Street. Even when saloon keepers were indicted, they escaped punishment. Citizens organized a Law and Order League to bring things under control, but the man they employed was a party to the conditions he was hired to correct.

The most dangerous problem, however, was that of fire protection. The city had grown more rapidly than its water system or its provisions for firefighting. Disastrous fires in 1900, 1902, and 1903 revealed the town's vulnerability. The first fire destroyed the seminary building at Wittenberg with a total loss of building and contents. The fire burned for three hours because water pressure was too low to be effective. The second fire was at the East Street Shops on February 10, 1902. The fire destroyed Whitely's great factory block, affecting ten businesses and putting hundreds out of work. Only one of the ten resumed operation.

In 1901 the Krell-French Piano Company had purchased the north wing of the massive Whitely structure. They had just completed remodeling the building and held a community open house. The factory was to produce 12,000 pianos a year. A request in 1900 for extension of a water main and installation of fire hydrants had been turned down by city council. When the fire came, low water pressure, inadequate equipment, and bad judgment at the scene added up to a total loss of the new plant.

On February 19, 1903, a third fire occurred in the cen-

Champion workers are depicted dragging a hose reel in a drill about 1900. Fire protection in Springfield was inadequate due to low water pressure and poor equipment. CCHS

ter of town. It destroyed Black's Opera House, Mitchell Brothers Plumbing Store, the Tibbetts Building, the Fountain Square Theater, the Junior Order United American Mechanics Hall, Kaufman's Clothing Store, and the YMCA. Three people died and several were injured. There were recriminations about the efficiency of the fire-fighting team and judgments at the scene.

Another critical unattended issue that exploded with unbelievable violence was that of race relations. Springfield's population had been growing steadily, but the black male population had been growing even more rapidly as blacks from the South came north looking for jobs. Increasing numbers registered to vote, organized the Negro Protective Party, and sought to create a balance of power between Republicans and Democrats. The issues were equal-education opportunities, the right to be nominated for political office, jobs, and social interaction.

The newly remodeled factory of the Krell-French Piano Company, purchased the year before from the Whitely interests, was lost in the East Street Shops fire on February 10, 1902. The doomed factory was to produce 12,000 pianos a year. Low water pressure, inadequate equipment, and bad judgment at the fire scene added up to a complete loss of the new facility. CCHS

Above
An entire block, including Kaufman's Clothing Store and Black's Opera House (on the second floor of the building on the northwest corner of Main Street and Fountain Avenue), was destroyed by fire on February 19, 1903. Three people died and several more were injured. CCHS

Opposite
Springfield proved disastrously vulnerable to fire at the turn of the century. Horse-drawn apparatus, seen here at Engine House Four about 1890, could be crippled by epizootic, a form of equine distemper. At one time teams of oxen were used to pull equipment because nearly all the fire horses were too sick for service. CCHS

Todd observed, "This animosity on the part of whites toward blacks is strong and growing; and on the part of the blacks is a growing jealousy of rights, real or supposed." He cited problems in the schools, even though segregation ended twenty years earlier. A growing sentiment among black clergy and professional men for black candidates for political office was evident. Most aggravating, however, was the job situation. Employers seldom employed a black man for anything other than common, unskilled labor. It was very difficult for an educated black to find employment. Since integration black teachers were no longer employed. There was little association of the two races, and there was growing discontent about this isolation.

The situation culminated in a lynching and race riot in 1904 and another in 1906. Twice in three years the Ohio

National Guard had to restore order. In the second riot townsmen burned the Levee, a predominantly black area where black and white vice flourished. The accumulation of problems finally prompted the citizens and leaders to take action. Before the turn of the century citizens had reformed the city council in hopes of improving conditions, making it a legislative body with a separate Board of Public Affairs to perform executive functions and coordinate autonomous departments.

In 1913 the state legislature passed Home Rule, which authorized twenty-five cities to function under city charters. Springfield voters adopted a charter authorizing a commission-manager form of government by a two-to-one margin. Under the new government the city commission was composed of five local residents who hired a professional manager to operate the city.

Local leaders favored the system. It provided for management like that of a successful business. The commission was the city's board of directors, and the manager was its chief executive officer. The heads of departments reported to him, and city employees were selected on the basis of Civil Service merit procedures. Businessmen themselves ran for election to the commission, and for many years the city's most successful local citizens served on the council.

Under Home Rule taxes were lowered and public services improved, debt was paid off, overhead costs were reduced, the fire and street cleaning departments were mo-

Left
In 1913 this group of men drafted the charter that gave Springfield its city commission-manager form of government. The innovation led to lower taxes and improved public services. Pictured seated, from left, are: Dr. Charles G. Heckert; J. Howard Littleton; Stewart L. Tatum, president; John J. Hoppes, treasurer; and John W. Garner. Standing, from left, are: Glenn M. Whitesell, assistant secretary; William C. Hewitt; H.S. Kissell; W.S. Thomas; J.E. Bowman; James H. Augustus, vice-president; Robert I. Netts; Francis C. Link; Willis M. Wise; Charles Bauer; T.J. Kirkpatrick; and George L. Rinkliff, secretary. CCHS

Above
Springfield's city commission brought better management, lower taxes, and improved public services. Members of Springfield's first city commission met in 1914. From left around the table are: P.J. Shouvlin; C.F. McGilvrary; B.J. Westcott; J.H. Hoppess; August Beaupain, secretary; and Elza McKee, city clerk. CCHS

torized, new grade school buildings were constructed, three new neighborhood playgrounds were established, and nearly one million dollars was expended for street and sewer improvements.

The first commission hired the most experienced man in the profession of city management, a man who, in fact, invented the commission-manager idea in 1908 in Staunton, Virginia—Charles E. Ashburner. This was the man Springfield's commission wanted for their manager, and Ashburner accepted.

As Springfield set about the task of dealing with problems head-on, the town's optimism and high spirits became apparent. The Champion City, The City of Roses (because of a manufacturing florist which became the world's largest developer of new rose varieties), The Home City, saw itself as a city with an exciting present and a promising future.

New construction showed city optimism—the domed high school in classic Federal style; the Springfield Building and Loan Association in modified Ionic; the Memori-

al Hall, an auditorium seating 2,700, which opened in 1916, saluting Civil and Spanish-American War veterans; the Big Four and Pennsylvania Railroad stations; and *The Springfield Daily News* building in the architectural style of the nation's great newspapers, sturdy, institutional. The *Daily News* was formed in 1905, a consolidation of *The Press Republic* and *The Daily Democrat.* The roots of *The Press Republic* reached back to the first newspaper, *The Farmer,* in 1817. The architecture of the new building made the paper an institution, similar in stature to banks, schools, churches, and government.

In this new spirit of optimism, the Commercial Club advertised Springfield's attractions to those looking for a place to locate. The new city government was a major selling point. The turnaround reflected the national reform spirit. States were adopting the direct primary, the initiative and referendum, and the direct election of senators. The national banking system had been reformed with the creation of the Federal Reserve System. Increasing numbers of states were adopting prohibition and women's suffrage. The reform spirit dissipated during World War I, after which a period of conservatism and reaction set in.

America moved steadily toward entrance into the war. As early as 1914, the United States economy, including Springfield's, was bolstered by Allied orders. By 1915 the nation enjoyed war-related prosperity, and Americans leaned toward the Allied cause. For the quarter of the population with German ancestors there were problems. German submarine warfare led to the sinking of neutral vessels and the killing of noncombatants. These events steadily eroded latent support. The Zimmerman plot, in which Germany asked Mexico to join the central powers in the event of war with the United States, added fuel to the fire. In April 1917 Congress passed a war resolution and America went to war.

Springfield High School dropped German as a foreign language, and students switched to Spanish. In the nation's war hysteria, Springfield's many citizens of German descent and the presence of a college with a German name—Wittenberg—caused many to regard it as a pro-German city. There had been a revival of German culture in the closing decades of the nineteenth century, and Wit-

tenberg and Springfield had been caught up in the discovery of German music, gymnasiums, and physical education. The town had embraced the kindergarten and German singing societies, like the Liedertafel. When the war came, neither the town nor the college—in spite of large enlistments, devotion to war production, and the purchase of war bonds—could escape harassment.

To reverse the tide of prejudice Dr. Charles G. Heckert, president of Wittenberg, and Harry S. Kissell, president of the board of realtors, went to New York to invite Theodore Roosevelt to Springfield and Wittenberg to speak at a war bond rally, and testify to the community's loyalty. He agreed to come. Speaking in Hiller Chapel at Wittenberg, Roosevelt said he wanted to come to Springfield to inculcate doctrines of true Americanism. "I decline to recognize any discrimination...because of the creed any man professes or because of diverse nationalities." The judgment, he implied, should be upon a man's service, sympathies, and actions, and those of Wittenberg and Springfield were above reproach and deserved commendation.

Roosevelt also spoke in the city, encouraging local citizens to continue war support. Later, in *Cosmopolitan Magazine,* he referred to the patriotism and loyalty of the citizens of Springfield and the students and faculty at Wittenberg.

Above
The Springfield Daily News building on Washington Street presides in the background as some of its staff members take an opportunity to inspect a new police car in this photo from the late 1920s. CCHS

Below
President Theodore Roosevelt came to Springfield during World War I to dispell the prejudice toward persons and things German. Roosevelt is pictured leaving Recitation Hall after lauding Wittenberg circa 1917. From the left are: Charles G. Heckert, President of Wittenberg; Ray Drenning, Springfield detective; President Roosevelt; Harry S. Kissell, Springfield business leader; and Harry Boswell; Springfield police inspector. From the Wittenberg University Archives

Above
A wagon of the Beckley & Myers Ice & Fuel Company paused in front of the Springfield City Building in 1912. The company delivered ice for refrigeration in the summer and coal for fireplaces and furnaces during the winter. Flags and bunting indicate that it may have been the Fourth of July. CCHS

Top, right
The Clark County Courthouse, completed in 1881, is pictured circa 1916. CCHS

Many citizens worked in factories and in volunteer service supporting soldiers in nearby camps. Wittenberg became a training center for army officers and supplied chaplains for military units in the area. War bond efforts were oversubscribed. Hundreds of citizens served directly in the armed services.

One Springfield soldier, Frank D. Kronk, kept a diary of his experiences with the army from the time he arrived at Camp Sherman in Ohio to his return to the United States and home. Many Springfielders accompanied him, and his tale was one which many could recall: the crossing on the British ship *Leicestershire* with its Hindu crew and meals of rabbit and marmalade; vigilance in looking for submarines; arrival in Europe; the sorry state of women and children in the war-ravaged lands; rain and mud; "cooties" and vermin; the friendliness of the people in France and Germany; card games and relaxation with the YMCA; casualties and suffering; the expense—in one day's entry Kronk noted: "We fired over 5,000 shots, over half-a-million dollars"; and finally the Armistice; the prisoners of war; the women and children coming out of hiding to return to what was left of their homes; and occupation duty in Germany.

He described the American counteroffensive at Verdun: "Our infantry went over the top at 7 a.m. and captured

several prisoners. We are firing a shell a minute. Gun is red hot. Have a gang with buckets throwing water and laying wet sacks over them. Barrage lasted seven-and-a-half hours." His diary entries followed the battle for several days.

Another Springfielder, Corporal Leon Roth, told a happier story. Roth was a dispatch rider with the 319th Signal Battalion, and at 4 a.m. on November 11, 1918, he was sent to Marshal Foch's French army headquarters to pick up a message and deliver it to American headquarters. "Hurry this to headquarters and ride like hell," he was told, "This is one message that must go through." Roth rode his motorcycle with the thunder of guns all about him. "You've brought us the best news we've heard," he was told upon arrival, "the war is over." Roth had delivered the news of the Armistice, hammered out overnight in Marshal Foch's railway car. At 11 a.m. firing ceased.

Rapid demobilization brought troops home faster than the nation's capacity to absorb them into the work force. There was no GI Bill or program of services to assist in rehabilitation. Most were just delighted to be back and relied upon continuing prosperity to accommodate them.

Springfield still boasted more than 200 diverse industries, and while the cancellation of war orders affected some, it did not affect all. Two businesses were emerging as mainstays of the local economy—Crowell-Collier Publishing and International Harvester—and both made postwar news.

Since 1912 International Harvester had been involved with the federal government in antitrust negotiations. The litigation covered six years and resulted in 10,000 pages of records, including the testimony of 1,200 persons. International Harvester was accused of being a monopoly. Finally in 1918 the company entered into a consent decree that threatened Springfield. It was to dispose of the Osborne, Milwaukee, and Champion lines and the plants where they were made. Pursuant to this agreement the company sold Champion Reaper to B.F. Avery of Louisville, Kentucky, but Avery did not want the Springfield plant. Eventually the federal government agreed to let IH operate its Springfield plant, provided they did not make harvesters. Since IH was beginning to make trucks, the decision was made to convert the Springfield operation from making harvesters to trucks.

Crowell Publishing Company did not face such difficulties in its expansion. In 1915 the company purchased *The American Magazine,* which had started life as *Frank Leslie's Popular Monthly* in the mid-1850s. After the war, in 1919, Crowell's acquired *Collier's Magazine,* which had become famous for photojournalism. The company name was changed to the Crowell-Collier Publishing Company. Collier's had become known for journalistic crusades against patent medicines, William Randolph Hearst, Grapenuts cereal, and the International Harvester monopoly. Ironically the magazine was now to be published in a major center for International Harvester.

Crowell-Collier executives in New York decided to enlarge their Springfield plant to 350,000 square feet of printing and office space and raise the number employed to 2,000. Detroit, Toledo, and Ironton (DT&I) rail lines would run into the plant to deliver the 40,000 tons of paper and one million pounds of ink consumed annually. The plant shipped an average of ten carloads of magazines daily.

A third local enterprise entered a new phase of growth in the postwar era—Wittenberg College. The college grew in resources, academic prestige, and athletic prowess. In 1906 industrialist Andrew Carnegie had included Wittenberg on his list of beneficiaries. He gave Wittenberg Carnegie Science Hall and allowed the faculty to join the teachers' retirement fund that he had created through the Carnegie Foundation. Several local families had also become benefactors. The Zimmerman family gave the school its Zimmerman Library before the turn of the century. John W. Bookwalter endowed a chair of philosophy, and Dr. and Mrs. Samuel F. Greenawalt established the Ross Mitchell Professorship of Religion, honoring one of Wittenberg's and Springfield's most generous citizens. In 1921 the Rockefeller Foundation gave Wittenberg a significant endowment gift to support faculty salaries. The school's academic prestige advanced because of generous gifts, but also because the school attracted outstanding faculty members and capable students.

For many citizens, however, the school was better known because of athletics. Wittenberg had played intercollegiate football since 1892 and intercollegiate basketball since 1902. But in 1918, 1919, and 1920 Wittenberg was un-

defeated in football. A Wittenberg Stadium Company was founded by rooters, and in 1923 the Wittenberg stadium was dedicated. Five years later Wittenberg joined Miami, Ohio, Cincinnati, Ohio Wesleyan, and Denison universities to establish the Buckeye Athletic Conference. The teams brought excitement to local crowds and forged an alliance between town and college focused on athletics. A capital funds campaign raised $300,000 to build a new health and physical education building complete with basketball court and swimming pool.

Although IH, Crowell's, and Wittenberg were the largest local enterprises there were a couple of hundred others, and new ones continued to form. In 1925 Ralph Hollenbeck, Frank J. Braun, and Allen McGregor, local businessmen and bankers, founded the Credit Life Insurance Company, destined to become a giant in its field. Earlier, in 1921, Edwin D. Parker of the W.T. Parker Company had begun making lawn sweepers. In 1928 Joseph Shouvlin sold the Superior Gas Engine Company to the National Supply Company.

By 1924 over 20,000 men and nearly 6,000 women were employed. Women's jobs covered a broader range than ever before. They were now factory workers, office clerks, servants, stenographers and typists, teachers, bookkeepers, cashiers, accountants, saleswomen, dressmakers, milliners, laundresses, store clerks, housekeepers, telephone operators, and nurses. Others kept boarding houses and served as midwives. There were female musicians and music teachers and college professors. There were three female physicians, three female clergy, nine authors, editors, and reporters, and eight artists, sculptors, or art teachers.

In 1924 the Commercial Club became the Chamber of Commerce. The year before the Springfield Foreman's Club was founded by Walter V. Edwards of the YMCA. The group later became the Springfield Management Association, affiliated with the National Management Association.

These groups, together with a growing number of service clubs, provided an invaluable civic network. As population grew and the city's social and economic life expanded, such groups became increasingly important. The first service club was the Springfield Rotary Club, founded in 1914. Its membership policies allowed for one person from each field of business and industry and from each profession.

Culturally Springfield also continued to grow. In 1922 the Springfield Civic Orchestra was founded by Charles L. Bauer, a local industrialist with Bauer Brothers Company and a strong patron of local musical activities. In 1916 Bauer was instrumental in starting the Springfield Choral Society, which sponsored the annual Spring Music Festival. In 1927 the Springfield Civic Orchestra was reorganized as the Springfield Symphony Orchestra, a group

Above
In 1924 the Commercial Club became the Chamber of Commerce. The group bought the Lagonda Club (pictured to the right, during the late 1940s) for its offices. CCHS

Below
A.B. Graham (center), superintendent of schools, started the 4-H Club movement during the 1890s. Graham is pictured in 1902 with the eighth-grade class of Springfield Township. That same year The Ohio State University invited him to become supervisor of agricultural extension clubs for boys and girls, and he organized 4-H on a national basis. CCHS

Saloons were open day and night, and the Dry League, pictured in 1913, wanted them closed. From left, seated, are members: Dr. Clarence Gardener, pastor of the First Lutheran Church; Frank Krapp, judge of Common Pleas Court; Dr. V.G.A. Tressler, professor at Hamma Divinity School; Stuart Tatum; and William F. Bivette, postmaster. From left, standing, are: C.H. Pierce; A.L. Slager; W.B. Patton, MD; Mr. Kelly; and O.F. Hypes. CCHS

that provided a regular season of concerts until the middle of the Great Depression, its last concert given April 29, 1935.

Generally life in postwar Springfield was lively and enjoyable. The flapper styles, the increasing number of movies and automobiles, and the fast life of speakeasies and cigarettes were apparent. Springfield's Golden Age continued after the war, livelier than before.

For all the city's urban and industrial progress, its roots were still in the soil of central Ohio. Symbolic of that origin, A.B. Graham, superintendent of Springfield schools, had started the 4-H Club movement in the basement of the Clark County Courthouse in the 1890s. He took his high school agricultural club there because the school board disapproved of his using class time to talk about better farming techniques and home management. In 1902 the Ohio State University invited Graham to become supervisor of agricultural extension clubs for boys and girls, and he organized the clubs on a national basis. They adopted the name 4-H, the four *h*'s standing for head, heart, hand, and health.

A second local schoolteacher, George Harrison Shull, made great contributions to world agriculture. Shull applied to become principal of Springfield High School in 1901. When he did not get the job, he entered the University of Chicago for further study of botany. Shull became an expert in plant genetics. In 1909, having discovered the basic principles of corn genetics, he made proposals for their practical use in the development of hybrid corn. By 1914 he was urging the application of the principles of plant and animal genetics to obtain maximum yields in all farm crops and animals. He pursued an outstanding career of research and writing that made him a world-renowned scholar in his field.

Springfield's deep roots in the agricultural community, however, also provided it with the first evidence that the prosperity of the Gay Nineties and the Roaring Twenties was ending. In 1921 America's farm prices collapsed. The agricultural depression involved many foreclosures and more and more farmers moved to the city looking for work. At the same time social tensions reemerged. In 1921 the Ohio National Guard came to Springfield to preserve order as new racial fighting erupted. Membership in the Ku Klux Klan grew. In 1923 the state Klan met in Springfield, staged a parade, and held a rally at the fairgrounds near the city's major black neighborhood.

As the '20s drew to a close, most citizens in Springfield still enjoyed a fulfilling, prosperous life, but the optimism of prewar reform had given way to an era of conservatism. Just beneath the surface lurked serious problems that would soon engulf the community.

6 *From Depression to War*

"With an aching heart I looked for the environments which nourished my love of nature, but they were not there." In his diary young Walter Brigham Evans, Jr., described the changes that had taken place around Springfield as the town grew and the county prospered in the years preceding the Great Depression. Specifically, he was describing the Mad River Valley west and northwest of town in 1929. The only cedar swamp south of Michigan, he lamented, had been sacrificed in the name of progress. The beautiful valley wilderness was now gone.

Evans confided to his diary that as he rode out St. Paris Pike where it crossed Mad River he could see how the "conservancy plan" had replaced swampy woods with fields of wheat and corn. "One wonders," he mused, "in the midst of the evil of farm overproduction, why the farmers want to increase their cultivated areas."

Others might well have raised the same question. While many Americans marked the beginning of the Great Depression with the stock market crash of 1929, for those on the farms and in towns whose business depended upon the farmer, hard times had started earlier. The bottom had fallen out of farm markets as early as 1921, and a growing number of foreclosures forced more and more farmers to move to Springfield and seek work.

The 1929 stock market crash affected some Springfielders dramatically, and the months following were months of reassessment and reappraisal. Few, however, foresaw either the depth or the length of the economic calamity that was coming. Yet 1929 became a year of transition, from the glitter of the Roaring Twenties to an era of great social change. In the years following 1929 the citizens of Springfield and elsewhere experienced a narrower perspective, a concentration on the problems of personal survival.

Few noticed the new world emerging around them. For most the Depression developed gradually, almost imperceptibly. Springfielders, in fact, began the year 1930 with optimism. The banner headline in *The Springfield Daily News* for New Year's Day 1930 was "Prosperity Forecast for New Year," and with stories datelined Washington, D.C., and Columbus, Ohio, local residents were told to expect continued economic progress. Both government and industry leaders talked optimistically. Analysts called the stock market crash the outstanding economic event of 1929, but opinions on the meaning of the collapse were varied. While there were signs of recession preceding the crash, most felt that corrective measures were being taken.

Locally, retail merchants noted that they had experienced a strong economic year with a particularly good Christmas shopping season. All were restocking their shelves with the expectation that spring business would be brisk. Business was good, if not spectacular, and credit purchases were being paid for on time.

A panel of local leaders heard a presentation by an officer of the Cleveland Trust Company and then gave their own predictions. The speaker highlighted four elements in the economic picture. First, industry was slowing down, particularly autos, iron and steel, and construction. Second, the stock market crash had affected many of the nation's investors. Third, interest rates were declining. Fourth, the administration in Washington was organizing nationwide efforts to sustain business activity and avoid

Opposite
Army Air Corps Cadets trained on the Wittenberg campus during World War II. A group of cadets is pictured in 1943 in front of Ferncliff Hall as they prepared to run to assembly. From the Wittenberg University Archives

unemployment. The result, he said, was that 1930 would get off to a slow start but gain pace, turning out to be an average year.

Local reactions were generally optimistic. Even if there was to be a depression nationally, Springfield had a good chance of escaping it as it had before. S.B. Mathewson, secretary and manager of the Chamber of Commerce, noted that if everyone cooperated to promote local public works, any slack in employment could be provided for until the economy turned around. Local bankers were equally sure that the extensive construction planned in the area would tide it over.

J.L. Shriver, Clark County agricultural extension agent, was also optimistic. The "silk shirt" days of World War I were gone, he said, but practical farmers would make as much in 1930 as they did in 1929, barring crop failure or livestock disease. Only Chester A. Baldwin, president of the Springfield Trades and Labor Assembly, seemed less than optimistic. If, however, local industry paid higher wages and adopted the eight-hour day and the forty-four-hour work week to spread work around, Baldwin saw no reason to expect prolonged difficulty.

Harry S. Kissell, local realtor and member of a commission appointed by the National Chamber of Commerce at President Hoover's request to study business conditions, was generally optimistic, but he worried about unemployment. It was very important, he said, for employers to furnish as much employment as possible to as many men as possible. If they didn't or couldn't, he said, things would begin to unravel.

Unravel they did, nationally and locally, as the nation slipped into the longest and deepest economic downturn in its history.

One of the results of the Great Depression was that the city's population growth halted. While population had been increasing more than ten percent per decade since the turn of the century, it grew only about three percent in the 1930s, from 68,743 in 1930 to 70,662 in 1940. County population grew from 90,936 to 95,647 in the same period of time. From then on population in the county grew at a faster rate than that of the city.

The booming industries that had attracted ever-growing numbers of newcomers to Springfield were no longer booming, and the number of jobs diminished. There was further loss of local control as more and more owners sold to out-of-town companies. Local movers and shakers, beset with their own personal and economic problems, were less able to give time and energy and resources for local activities. For some, their fortunes had vanished overnight. Others were hard pressed. Nationally, stock market values lost seventy-five billion dollars in the first two years of the crisis. Many local businessmen had foreseen their growing dependence on widespread markets, but they had not foreseen worldwide economic collapse and its resultant impact on the life and economy of Springfield. Factories closed or operated on reduced shifts. Wages and salaries were reduced. Banks closed. Foreclosures on businesses and homes were commonplace. Some people reverted to a barter system, offering services for food or supplies.

It was an era of great misery and unemployment. The Works Progress Administration (WPA) provided jobs for a number of people on streets and highways. Private enterprise provided additional jobs in projects like the new Wittenberg field house, which opened in 1930. Govern-

ment provided the new city hospital at High Street and
Burnett Road in 1932, after months of argument over
twenty possible sites in all parts of town. The new post
office was also constructed in 1932, and Evans Stadium
was built by the city schools in 1936. Culturally the city
marked time. The symphony closed as the Civic Theater
opened.

An unsung but bold response to the times came from
the Young Woman's Mission. In 1935, under the leadership of housewives Margaret Greenawalt and Fanny
Winger, the group opened a mothers' health clinic, the
ninth birth-control clinic in Ohio and a forerunner of
planned parenthood in the area. At the time such activities were illegal in Ohio. Interest in family planning and
birth control grew with the hard times, since feeding ex-
tra mouths was to be avoided if possible.

Local athletics experienced a setback in 1929 when the
athletic director at Ohio University accused Wittenberg of
professionalism in sports. Others in the six-team Buckeye
League of Wittenberg, Cincinnati, Ohio University, Denison, Miami, and Ohio Wesleyan echoed the charge. Wittenberg president Rees Edgar Tulloss found that local
alumni boosters were violating recruitment and scholarship rules. Tulloss cracked down, but was unable to
avoid a public scandal. The college vowed to operate its
athletic programs henceforth so as to avoid any hint of
irregularity.

Local sports enthusiasts turned their attention to other
matters. The Springfield baseball team in the Central
League was in danger of folding. Springfield had been
playing a regular schedule against Dayton, Fort Wayne,
Akron, and other cities, but couldn't post sufficient funds
for the new season. Joseph C. Shouvlin took the lead in
organizing a group to sell ten thousand advance tickets.
Happily, they succeeded.

The Battle of Piqua sesquicentennial in 1930 was an
equally joyous development for local residents. Local historians had obtained a monument for the site in 1924—a
sculptured obelisk designed by Charles Keck of New
York and paid for by a state appropriation of ten thousand dollars. In return the Clark County Historical Society deeded the site to the state of Ohio. In 1928 Governor
A. Victor Donahey appointed a George Rogers Clark
Memorial Commission. The commission recommended reenactment of the famous battle on August 8, 1930, state
purchase of the site of the battle and birthplace of Tecumseh for a state park, and construction of a museum in
the form of a frontier fort.

In 1930 the Ohio Revolutionary War Memorial Commission acquired the additional lands to create the park.
In the fall the state scheduled various ceremonies commemorating Ohio's Revolutionary War past, culminating
in the mock reenactment of the Battle of Piqua. It was a

HERE
GENERAL
GEORGE ROGERS
CLARK

WITH HIS KENTVCKY SOLDIERS
DEFEATED AND DROVE
FROM THIS REGION
THE SHAWNEE INDIANS
AVGVST 8 1780

THVS AIDING TO MAKE
THE NORTHWEST TERRITORY
PART OF THE VNITED STATES

*A monument to George Rogers Clark and his soldiers for bravery in the
Battle of Piqua was erected by the Clark County Historical Society and
the State of Ohio in a ceremony on August 8, 1924. A detail of the
monument proclaimed that Clark's efforts helped "make the Northwest
Territory part of the United States." CCHS*

gala celebration, and large crowds watched the colorful event. A few years later the WPA constructed a dam and created an artificial lake to grace the park and battlefield. The park commissioners named the addition after A.D. Hosterman, longtime county official and park superintendent.

By the summer of 1932 a bedraggled bonus army encamped in a different park, Cliff Park, below the Wittenberg campus. The army was on its way to Washington, D.C., to demand bonuses for World War I veterans. Springfield workmen were caught up in the national trend of sit-down strikes, and workers at the Springfield Metallic Casket Company quit work and took over the plant. Labor was growing desperate. Some industrialists were also growing desperate. These industrialists felt a chief obligation to their workers to meet the payroll, and they were increasingly unable to do so. It was a trying time for workers and owners, and all the traditional remedies seemed useless.

Not every business suffered equally, however. The Crowell-Collier Publishing Company maintained a steady level of production and employment as the nation stayed home and read magazines. The demand for *Collier's*, *Women's Home Companion*, and *The American Magazine*—and for the features, fiction stories, and cartoons they contained—kept the presses on High Street humming and provided steady employment for hundreds of Springfield men and women. The volume of magazines mailed to subscribers around the nation made the Springfield Post Office one of the busiest in the state.

The Chakeres Theater chain grew and spread across Ohio and into adjacent states as the movies provided people with an inexpensive escape from their troubles. Cash prizes and other premiums on "Bank Night" (where drawings were made at intermission), and the double and triple feature with selected short subjects, made movie going more exciting and an even better bargain. Nevertheless plans for a new theater at Main and Fisher streets were shelved indefinitely.

The automobile also offered new business and employment opportunities, such as repair shops and filling stations. Paul Deer founded the Bonded Oil Company, opening his first station in Urbana in 1932. A new economy based on oil was beginning. In December 1933 the city's electric streetcars were replaced by a new gasoline-powered city bus system. Other new businesses were started by brave souls willing to bet on the local economy. John Kuhns founded the Kuhns Controlled Concrete Company in 1935, and Harry Leventhal purchased the Vining Broom Company in 1939 and was soon joined by his brother Fred Leventhal, who became a most public-spirited citizen.

In the long run national magazines, radio and movie

Above
Springfield student Charles Lemen, pictured circa 1928, was a staff announcer for Wittenberg's radio station WCSO. The transmitter was built by faculty members of the physics department. Name entertainers often appeared on late night broadcasts, after they had finished their performances in local theaters. WCSO was heard across the United States and in Canada and Mexico. In 1931 its powerful transmitter was sold to WJR in Detroit and used in early experiments in television. From the Wittenberg University Archives

entertainment, and the automobile changed local cultural activities. One of the more subtle developments of the depression years was the growth of a national popular culture, which quietly supplanted more localized activities. Magazines and movies expanded horizons, gave Americans a shared popular culture, and got them used to a higher literary and artistic standard. Local efforts often suffered by comparison. Radio and the movies gave Springfielders and the nation national stars and songs.

Springfield tuned in to WCSO, the Wittenberg College radio station, the first in the city. Residents also tuned in to WLW in Cincinnati, WJR in Detroit, KDKA in Pittsburgh, and half a dozen other stations whose broadcast schedules were printed daily in local newspapers. Networks of stations brought "Amos 'n Andy," Fred Allen, George Burns and Gracie Allen, and other stars regularly into Springfield homes. Programs as varied as the "Renfro Valley Barn Dance" and the "Carnation Contented Hour" appealed to segments of the Springfield market.

The automobile established a closer social and business connection between Springfield and other nearby communities. Expanded and improved concrete streets and roads made travel by car faster and more convenient than ever. Increased travel broadened cultural and moral, as well as geographic, horizons and set the stage for ending community self-containment. In 1930 George Click owned the first "radio-equipped auto" in town, one that made "long journeys seem short." Roads which once brought the world to Springfield's doors increasingly took Springfielders to far-flung places.

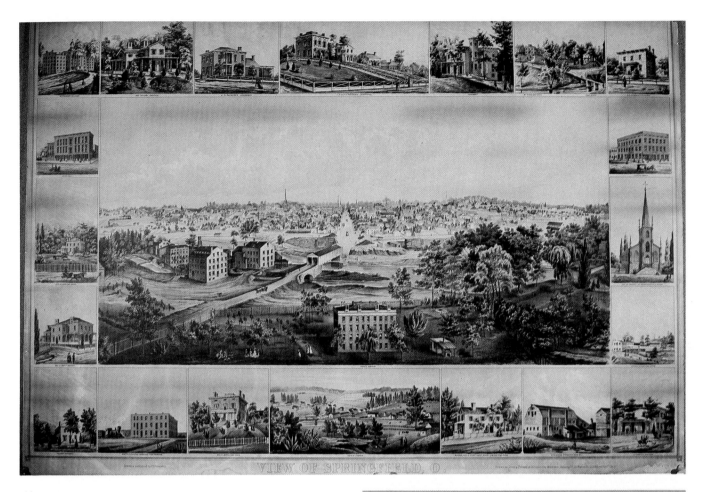

Above
This 1850 view of Springfield, Ohio, looks south toward the female seminary. The seminary, later Northern School, is now the site of the Springfield Board of Education offices. In the center of the picture is Limestone Street, and Wittenberg University is located today in the area to the right. Surrounding the central view are other notable buildings in Springfield. CCHS

Above
The Springfield esplanade and fountain, flanked by the Arcade Hotel on the left and the City Building on the right, are pictured as they appeared about 1890. Today the new City Building is located diagonally across the street to the viewer's left. The City Market Building on the right is now the Elderly United Center. CCHS

Above
George Rogers Clark surveyed the upper Ohio in the early 1770s, fought
Indians in Governor Dunmore's expeditions of 1774, and with 200 men
captured the British fort of Vincennes in 1779. Clark later led nearly
1,000 backwoodsmen against the Shawnees in 1780 and defeated them in
the Battle of Piqua. Courtesy, Silson Club

Upper ellipse
Pierson Spining arrived in Springfield from New Jersey in 1812 and
achieved success as a merchant, shipping his goods overland from Philadelphia and New York to Pittsburgh, then by flatboat to Cincinnati,
and then overland to Springfield. In 1832 he brought the first piano to
Springfield for his family, shipping it over the same torturous route.
CCHS

Lower ellipse
Kentuckian Maddox Fisher arrived in Springfield in 1813 with $20,000
in his pocket. He invested in real estate, built a mill, and opened a store.
Fisher is credited with the formation of Clark County and getting
Springfield selected as the county seat in 1818. CCHS

Above
Samuel Shellabarger opposed slavery in the 1850s and advised Spring-fielders that only a free and enlightened people with a free press and Christian spirit could preserve the nation. Shellabarger was elected to Congress in 1860 on the Republican ticket. CCHS

Below
The Hertzler House, a three-story brick dwelling of early American de-sign, is located on the rim of a valley several miles west of Springfield in what is now George Rogers Clark Park. It was built about 1850 by Daniel Hertzler, distiller and mill owner. CCHS

Above
Springfield's agricultural orientation was evidenced by means other than the manufacture of farm machinery. An active Agricultural Society was formed to meet the needs of farmers, and this silk ribbon identified members at the 1854 Clark County Fair. The year before, the society purchased a ten-acre fairground site south of town. CCHS

Above
This detail is from a poster that announced the partnership of Whitely, Fassler, and Kelly, formed in 1857 when Kelly supplied needed capital to the two inventors. Kelly withdrew from the company in 1881. CCHS

Right
This colorful 1883 catalog of P.P. Mast & Company extolled the products of the Buckeye Agricultural Works—grain drills, seeders, and cultivators. CCHS

This flamboyant circa 1889 poster for the Warder, Bushnell, and Glessner Company illustrated President Benjamin Harrison cutting the White House lawn with a Champion reaper as his cabinet looked on. CCHS

Above
The YMCA has been a positive force in Springfield since it was organized the summer of 1854. From the beginning it received the support and goodwill of the town's leaders by promoting the "social and religious well-being of its members." Stores and shops closed early on YMCA meeting nights so that young employees could participate. This building was built by the YMCA in 1901, and was partially destroyed in the fire that consumed Black's Opera House on February 19, 1903. From the F. Kenneth Dickerson Collection

Above
"Mother" Elizabeth Stewart, a Springfield housewife, began her crusade against alcohol shortly after the Civil War and became a nationally-known leader in the Women's Christian Temperance Union. CCHS

Above
David L. Snyder (pictured circa 1895), who had been associated with the Victor Rubber Company, and his brother John donated land to Springfield for a park in 1895. CCHS

Above
Springfield philanthropist John Snyder is pictured in 1895. The 225 acres he and his brother donated to Springfield became Snyder Park. CCHS

Below
The Warder Free Public Library building was dedicated in 1890 and is still in operation today. It is another Richardson Romanesque structure and an Ohio landmark. From the F. Kenneth Dickerson Collection

Above
Springfield began the last year of the nineteenth century by honoring Asa S. Bushnell for his four years of service as the Governor of Ohio. This embossed memento from the reception and banquet held January 10, 1900, carries a picture of the governor, the state capitol, and the state and national seals. CCHS

Right
A beautiful stained-glass window from the offices of the Warder, Bushnell, and Glessner Company proudly announced they manufactured "reapers, mowers, and self binders." The window is now on display at the Clark County Historical Society Museum. CCHS

Left
In 1924 McGregor's declared Springfield "the greatest rose-producing center in the world" and gave a free rose to anyone who was able to get a new customer to place a one-dollar order. CCHS

Bottom, left
Anti-German propaganda such as this 1917 poster drawn by William "Billy" Ireland of Columbus helped fan the flames of misunderstanding and prejudice toward all things German, creating problems for Springfield's citizens of German heritage and for Wittenberg College. CCHS

Bottom, right
One reason that Springfield was known as "The City of Roses" was its extensive seed and bulb industry. This 1915 catalog of the McGregor Brothers Company guaranteed delivery of "roses, shrubs, bulbs, or seeds . . . all over the world." CCHS

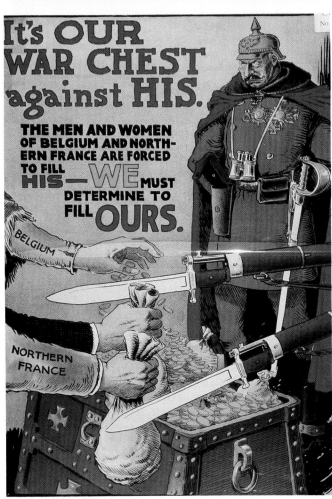

Industrialist Andrew Carnegie gave Wittenberg the Carnegie Science
Hall in 1906. From the Wittenberg University Archives

Above
Architect Ralph H. Harmon's drawing depicts the City Hospital, built in 1933. The government-funded project helped provide employment for many of Springfield's desperate workers. CCHS

Right
The Madonna of the Trail Monument honors the pioneer mother of covered wagon days. It is one of twelve such memorials placed by the Daughters of the American Revolution along the National Road in various states. Erected in 1928, it marked the point west of town upon which the National Road was completed in 1838. Courtesy, City of Springfield

Above
The Springfield Art Association built its first permanent home in 1967—the Springfield Art Center in Cliff Park. Six years later the building was enlarged to twice the orginal size. The association, formed in 1946, first had space in the Arcade Building, and later in an old home on East High Street. Courtesy, City of Springfield

Top
Lagonda Creek, *painted during the mid-nineteenth century by Godfrey Nicolas Frankenstein, is a fine example of the artist's work. Before his death in 1873, Frankenstein's views of Lagonda Creek were in collections in Cincinnati, Louisville, New York, Boston, and London. From the Wittenberg University Archives*

Above
Godfrey Nicolas Frankenstein was born in Germany in 1820, immigrated with his family to Cincinnati in 1831, and moved to Springfield in 1849. Frankenstein became a well-known painter of portraits and landscapes, and today his work is much sought after. The artist is pictured in a self-portrait from about 1850. CCHS

Above
The tractor-pull is a big event at the annual Clark County Fair. First held in 1854, the fair clings fast to its agricultural heritage with exhibits of farm machinery and animals and awards for homemaking and farming skills. Courtesy, Clark County Fair Board

Left
The arts are taken to the people in the City Building Plaza during Plazaffaire, sponsored by the Downtown Merchants Association and the Springfield Arts Council. Courtesy, Springfield Arts Council

Below
Thousands attend the free performances of the Springfield Arts Council's Summer Arts Festival each year. From the F. Kenneth Dickerson Collection

The lovely 225-acre Snyder Park, a gift to the people of Springfield from brothers John and David Snyder, is pictured in 1984. Courtesy, City of Springfield

Above
This view of downtown Springfield from the Core Renewal Block was taken circa 1980. Courtesy, City of Springfield

Right
Wittenberg University's new library was the visible result of a successful fund campaign completed in 1982. From the Wittenberg University Archives

Above
The Merchants and Mechanics Federal Savings and Loan, which built its
new building at the corner of Main and Limestone streets, is pictured
circa 1982. Courtesy, City of Springfield

Right
This stained-glass window was part of Springfield's exhibit in the Ohio
Building at the Columbian Exposition in Chicago in 1892. The window
is now on display in the Clark County Historical Society Museum.
CCHS

World War II ended the Depression and accelerated change. European unrest was brought home to Springfielders by wire-photo coverage in the *News and Sun,* by radio, and by *Movietone News* in theaters. Many heard Adolf Hitler's speeches to the German masses and saw Hitler and Benito Mussolini in the newsreels at the Regent or State theaters. The appeasements of British Prime Minister Neville Chamberlain and other leaders of Europe's democracies were viewed with both approval and apprehension by local audiences. The German invasion of Poland in 1939 signaled the start of a general conflict that most hoped America could avoid. Asian unrest, viewed as something of a side issue, culminated in the Japanese attack on Pearl Harbor on December 7, 1941, and America entered the war.

The attack on Pearl Harbor immediately brought the war to Springfield's door. The disbelief of local residents as they listened to radio accounts of the attack gave way to a sense of shock and grief as casualty reports came

During the early 1930s the Crowell-Collier mail room had a full staff hard at work. The publishing company maintained a steady level of employment during the Depression, as its customers stayed home and read. CCHS

through. Three Springfielders died in the attack: Seaman First Class William Welch, Seaman First Class C. Richard Ward, and Corporal John J. "Ted" Koch.

In the months before Pearl Harbor, Springfield industry had begun to revive with production for the Allies in Europe and for the United States defense program. With America's entrance into the war, there was an almost overnight revival of local industry and local business, leading soon to full employment and even a labor shortage.

Local industries made diesel engines for Liberty ships, engines for landing ship transport (LST) craft, M-5 half-tracks, torpedoes, military trucks, crawler tractors, airplane propellers, hub assemblies, airplane doors, bomb crates, artillery shells, walkie-talkie antennae, castings for B-17 Flying Fortresses, and calibration stands for the famous Norden Bombsight.

Air-raid drills and preparedness exercises were taken seriously as local residents, half proudly and half concerned, noted that the Dayton-Springfield area, with Wright-Patterson Air Force Base in between, would be one of the main air-raid targets in the country if the tide of war ran against America. News of the war was followed avidly in the newspapers, on radio, and through newsreels in the theaters. The automobile, even with rationed tires

Clarence C. "Prexy" Stoughton (center) initiated a period of renewed growth and building for Wittenberg University during his tenure as president from 1949 to 1963. Stoughton is pictured in 1954, setting the cornerstone for Weaver Chapel. From the Wittenberg University Archives

and gas, took more and more Springfielders to Dayton and Wright-Patterson fields to work.

Men, women, and children were caught up in the war effort. Students in local schools were fingerprinted for identification in case of air-raid attack and pressed to become members of the Red Cross, to collect cooking grease and tin cans, and to buy war stamps and war bonds. Parents were encouraged to work either in war plants or in volunteer programs and to plant victory gardens. Bundles for Britain, the USO, the Red Cross, and other groups enrolled civilians in the war effort. Wren's Department Store planted a victory garden in its display window on Main Street. To enable high school students to work, the school day was shortened. Students took part-time jobs and tasted the independence of earning their own money. For those without jobs whose parents were both at work, the YWCA and the YMCA developed after-school activity programs to keep them busy.

The major war service, however, was the armed forces, and thousands of area men and women enlisted and were drafted. The county's total war dead reached 376. Many more were wounded and hardly a family remained untouched. By the time the war ended, there was little enthusiasm left for a gala victory celebration.

The war's impact was clearly apparent at Wittenberg. In 1940 enrollment totaled 790. By 1941 enrollment dropped to 609. In 1943 it totaled only 295, mostly women. The senior class of 1945 listed 117 members, but 63 were on ac-

tive duty and 3 had been killed in action. Fifteen hundred alumni served in the armed forces, and sixty-five never returned from the battlefields.

During the war Wittenberg was selected as a site for a college training detachment of the Army Air Force. In February 1943, 350 cadets arrived on campus—the first of 2,800 who received training at Wittenberg. Approximately 700 cadets were present at all times, becoming a real presence in the Springfield community. Movie star and singer Gordon MacRae was just one of the thousands of uniformed cadets who spent part of his time at Wittenberg and in Springfield. The cadet program, plus the housing of women being trained in radar operation at nearby air fields, kept the institution going at a subsistence level.

When the war ended, however, the college was inundated with enrollments. The GI Bill enabled military personnel to enroll in the college or university of their choice, and Wittenberg, like schools across the country, faced a flood of older, war-experienced students that changed campuses immensely. From an enrollment low of 295 in 1943, Wittenberg expanded to 1,364 students in 1946, and the overflow was housed in war surplus army barracks on the football practice field and other locations around the campus.

As postwar enrollments burgeoned, Wittenberg president Rees Edgar Tulloss retired, ending the longest tenure of any of the school's presidents, from 1920 to 1949. He had presided over magnificent growth and expansion in the '20s, held the school together through the Depression of the '30s, and preserved its assets through the war for effective use when students returned.

Tulloss was succeeded by Clarence C. "Prexy" Stoughton from New York, who initiated a period of renewed growth and building. Prexy Stoughton became active in community affairs and conducted several successful fund-raising campaigns, attracting large gifts from private benefactors, the Ford Foundation, and the Springfield community. During his presidency Wittenberg built Weaver Chapel, Thomas Library, and several residence halls. Stoughton changed the school's name from Wittenberg College to Wittenberg University before retiring in 1963. Wittenberg's football and basketball teams reemerged to capture conference and national honors, and the university's choir toured Europe, Russia, and South America and sang on national radio.

With the end of the war came a baby boom, as returning servicemen took up the business of starting families as well as getting an education. Springfield soon had 10,000 babies. The demand for new schools was just ahead, and Superintendent of Schools E.E. Holt prevailed upon the community to get ready. Many new schools were built in all parts of town.

The large number of births also dramatized the need

for expanded hospital facilities. In 1946 Joseph C. Shouvlin headed a campaign to raise funds to start Mercy Hospital. It was built on North Fountain Boulevard, north of the Wittenberg campus on the site of the former Knights of Pythias Home, and opened in 1950.

There was also a housing shortage at the end of the war, and new housing developments were laid out north, south, and east of town. The price of building lots soared to an unbelievable $1,000 and more.

Amid all the postwar excitement there was a spirit of optimism and a concern for orderly progress, and much of the progress in schools, hospitals, and zoning resulted from the collective involvement of thousands of residents. In 1945 concerned citizens viewed the problems that would face the city at the war's end. They organized the Greater Springfield and Clark County Association (GSCCA) to mobilize local efforts to get various physical needs met, such as improved water and sewer systems, better fire equipment, and improvements in streets, which had been postponed during the war. Other members were concerned about schools and hospitals.

The GSCCA reached a membership of 8,000 and remained vigorously active for nearly a decade. In 1949 the group endorsed four energetic candidates for the City Commission— Paul G. Miller, Lawrence Schutte, Leon Yuell, and Lewis Rinewald. Their slogan was: "*Make Sure You're Right*—Miller, Schutte, Yuell, and Rinewald." All four were elected on a platform of city progress and improvement.

At the end of the war, Springfield opened its new airport south of town and converted the old one east of town into a fairgrounds for the revival of the Clark County Fair. Commercial air service began at the new airport but was short lived. The newer, larger planes focused service for the area at the Dayton Airport located twenty-five miles west of Springfield at Vandalia. In the fall of 1955 the Springfield Airport with its fine long runways became the home of the Ohio Air National Guard.

Interest in the arts also resumed with the end of the war. The Springfield Symphony had been revived in 1944. The first organized support for the symphony came with the organization of the Symphony Women's Association in 1945. In 1951 Evan Whalen became music director, and

Top, left
Springfield industrialist Joseph C. Shouvlin headed a fund to start Mercy Hospital in 1946. The hospital opened in 1950 on the site of the former Knights of Pythias Home at North Fountain Avenue, north of the Wittenberg campus. Courtesy, Springfield Newspapers, Inc.

Below
Thousands of Springfielders turned out to greet the campaign train of Dwight D. Eisenhower in 1952. As the train stopped at the Big Four Station, an excited crowd filled the intersection of Limestone and Washington streets. Courtesy, Springfield Newspapers, Inc.

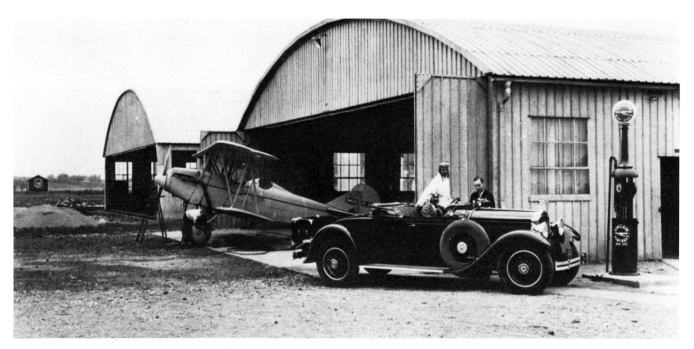

Above
The Clark County Fair took over the old Springfield Airport, east of Springfield, at the end of the war. In this circa 1947 photograph of the first fair at the new location runway markings are still visible! Courtesy, Springfield Newspapers, Inc.

Top
The Springfield Municipal Airport, established in 1928, is depicted during the mid-1930s. Accommodations included a school for flyers, hangers for private planes, repair service facilities, and a refueling station. Today the site is occupied by the Clark County Fairgrounds, and hangers provide space for exhibitors. CCHS

by 1955 the orchestra presented a five-concert season, youth concerts, and a pop concert.

In 1948 the Springfield Foundation was established for the purpose of financing local causes through charitable trusts for benevolent, educational, and cultural purposes in Clark County. The Springfield Foundation urged residents to "have a place in Springfield's history" by making gifts and bequests to support the quality of community life. In 1953, following a national trend, the United Appeals Fund of Clark County was founded, a forerunner of United Way. The idea was to pull together a variety of essential community service organizations that had been dependent upon separate fund drives and to have one major and well-supported drive for all causes at one time.

Clearly the residents of Springfield and Clark County came out of the war with the determination to make the community a better place to live, and their leaders focusd that enthusiasm on obtainable goals. The successes were many and community pride and enthusiasm grew. Problems that were bigger than the community, however, were less manageable.

Springfielders had expected the economy to sag as soon as the war ended, but it did not. Shortages of consumer goods had existed throughout the war, and pent-up demand was enormous. People had been earning good wages but had little to spend them on. Built-up savings and veterans bonuses fueled a recovery that overcame fears of returning depression. Factories were retooled for peacetime production to meet domestic demands and serve a world whose productive capacity had been greatly destroyed. The result was a boom economy for Springfield and Clark County.

Yet economic conditions were not all rosy. Too many dollars chasing too few goods led to runaway inflation and soaring profits. Labor, held off from strikes during the war effort, felt disadvantaged. There had been a bitter organizational drive by the United Auto Workers to organize International Harvester during the war. By 1946 labor unrest shut down the entire trucking industry. Within four years another angry strike closed the International Harvester plant for three months. The turmoil in the auto industry gave Springfield's labor scene more tension in the postwar decades than had ever existed in the prewar city. Local businessmen became concerned about the "two-tiered wage system" in which International Harvester workers earned so much more than workers in other plants and offices. Those interested in industrial expansion became concerned about the city's growing reputation for an imbalance in wages, strikes, and labor unrest.

Into this suffering industrial climate came a bombshell: the Crowell-Collier Publishing Company closed. The year was 1956. Collier's, which had been a mainstay of the local economy throughout the Depression and war years, was in trouble. The company was fighting a losing battle in the magazine publishing business and against television. Advertising was switching from magazines like the Crowell publications to new kinds of magazines such as Life and Look, but more than that to radio and television.

Even after terminating the publication of The American Magazine in mid-1956, the company was still losing $7.5 million per year. In December, while Springfielders were mostly unaware, the Crowell-Collier board met in New York to decide the fate of its magazine publishing business. The book-publishing division was netting five million dollars per year. If the loss side of the operation could be terminated, the company would return immediately to a condition of profitability. Late on a Saturday evening a decision was made: close the Springfield plant. On Monday 677 workers were fired. On Tuesday 200 more were let go. By the end of the week, the last 1,000 employees were terminated—five days before Christmas.

Springfield was shocked. The community was surprised that such a staunch local employer could be closed in less than a week, releasing nearly 2,000 employees just before the holidays. The action shook the community's confidence in itself and, less obviously, in American industry. Many of the printers, engravers, and other skilled workmen moved to other towns where printing was still a thriving business. Those who could not move or who were less skilled searched for alternative employment in the Springfield area. R.R. Donnelly and Company of Chicago, a major printing company, bought the plant, stripped it of its presses and equipment, and sought a suitable charity to give the building to in order to avoid further expense and taxation. Wittenberg considered the "gift" but turned it down. Donnelly then persuaded the University of Chicago to accept the gift, which it held empty for many years.

Neither Crowell-Collier Publishing Company nor Donnelly accepted responsibility for the impact their corporate decisions had on the local community or employees. For Springfield a decade of depression and stagnation ensued. The town that had put its faith in American industrial enterprise learned a hard lesson about absentee owners, one that would be repeated over and over again in other towns and cities of the industrial northeast.

The Crowell closing ended Springfield and Clark County's postwar decade, causing a psychological withdrawal comparable to that of the Great Depression. The community developed a heads-down, looking-at-its-feet view of the world. Local leadership had to concentrate on lifting spirits to get things moving again. It wasn't going to be easy.

7 Toward an Agenda for Tomorrow

When the Crowell-Collier Publishing Company closed down in 1956 it affected the 2,000 Crowell employees immediately and, gradually, all those whose jobs depended upon their weekly purchases. There was a more subtle effect on the younger generations entering the work force. Growing numbers of Springfield young people saw their futures outside town. The sons and daughters of middle- and upper-income families increasingly sought their fortunes elsewhere. Young men and women, who earlier would have remained in Springfield, moved away. Many new residents coming to town were from the South—particularly West Virginia. Farmers leaving the farm and blacks leaving the South moved to Springfield. There was growing conflict between groups of newcomers, and racial tensions increased.

There were other demographic trends at work, and the Crowell closing merely accentuated their effect. From around the 1870s, county residents living outside the city totaled approximately 20,000, while the city population grew to 20,000, then 30,000, 40,000, and continued to grow. County population meant Springfield population plus 20,000 until the late 1920s. In the 1930 census, county population, exclusive of the city, jumped to 22,000. It continued to grow and by 1950 was 33,000; in 1960 it reached 49,000. By 1970 the city population was 82,000, while county residents living outside the city limits totaled 75,000. By the 1980 census, county residents surpassed the city total—77,319 to 72,263.

The change was partly due to the growth of smaller villages in the county, like New Carlisle, but mostly it was because large housing developments like Northridge were built outside the city limits and not incorporated. It was another result of the phenomenon of the automobile, and it represented a major shift in political and economic

power. It also meant that Springfield was less and less the single focus of life and activity in the area.

These developments were characterized by the further emergence of regional and national culture over local culture—a trend most represented by television. In 1949 there were 2,500 television sets in the Greater Dayton area. By 1951 there were 215,000. Most area channels centered in Dayton and developed viewing areas totaling over one million sets in Ohio, Indiana, and Kentucky. Efforts to develop a commercial channel in Springfield, Channel 26, floundered. Later the channel was acquired by Miami Valley Christian Television, Inc. as special purpose and cable televison grew.

By the 1970s cable companies tied Springfield sets to stations in Cleveland, Cincinnati, Indianapolis, and Atlanta, as well as Dayton. Not until 1983 did one of the Dayton stations, WHIO-TV, open an official bureau in Springfield, as Springfield and Clark County became a large and important part of Dayton's megacity market area.

Another trend that accelerated in the 1970s was the acquisition of local firms by larger corporations and conglomerates. The process had been under way for a long time. By 1980 the number of locally owned firms had dwindled, especially among larger businesses. All but one local bank had been acquired by larger bank-holding companies from Cleveland and Columbus. These devel-

Opposite
Springfield Mayor Robert L. Burton had plans for a new city building in 1971. City commissioners are (from left) Roger Baker, Max E. Cordle, Mayor Burton, Robert Pyle, and Florence Heubner. City Manager Al Strozdas stands to the far right. Courtesy, City of Springfield

The biggest drive-away in International Harvester's history took place on May 28, 1968, when 946 units left the new truck plant in Springfield. Marshaled at the fairgrounds east of town, the vehicles are pictured lined up on State Route 41, over the as yet unopened I-70. Courtesy, Springfield Newspapers, Inc.

opments resulted in a further loss of influence over decisions affecting the local community and a reduction in the effectiveness of local initiative.

The city and county found themselves on a dividing line, a border between developments east and north and those west and south. The city's banks were based in Columbus and Cleveland. Its electric power company was the furthest southwest extension of an Akron-based Ohio Edison Company. Ohio Bell operated its telephones out of Columbus. Fuel gas was provided by Columbia Gas, whose territory ended at the western border of the county.

On the other hand the local newspapers were tied to Dayton and owned by Cox Newspapers, based in Atlanta. The area's major television stations were Dayton-based, and Springfield-Clark County news was incidental. For federal, judicial, and post-office services, the area also looked to Dayton.

Thus while politically, geographically, and commercially tied to the greater Dayton area, basic utilities and banking resources were increasingly oriented in the opposite direction. Therefore economic and industrial development, while it might be encouraged and promoted valiantly by local leadership, lacked the full power of a unified focus

of all energies and resources.

Not belonging totally to either the Dayton or the Columbus orbit, and determined to maintain a proud, if fading, independence, Springfield and Clark County planning proceeded in the corridor between the interests of their larger rivals. The divisions between townships, the city, and the county exacerbated the problems. The whole of Southwest Ohio, in fact, was characterized by an absence of effective regional planning and cooperation. Columbus, Dayton, and Cincinnati flexed their economic and political muscle with little or no attention to smaller communities in their areas of growth: among them, Hamilton, Middletown, Fairborn, Springfield, Xenia, New Carlisle, and London.

In an effort to counteract the lack of regional cohesiveness, which increasingly characterized the Dayton-Miami Valley area, colleges and universities in 1967 established the Dayton-Miami Valley Consortium. Institutional mem-

Neil A. Armstrong (Left), the first man to land on the moon, was awarded Wittenberg's honorary Doctor of Science degree by President G. Kenneth Andeen in 1969. From the Wittenberg University Archives

bers included: Wittenberg University and Clark Technical College from Springfield, and Urbana College, Antioch College, Wilmington College, Sinclair Community College, Central State University, Wilberforce University, University of Dayton, Wright State University, Cedarville College, and the Air Force Institute of Technology. Associate corporate members included: the Mead Corporation, the Kettering Foundation, Monsanto Research Corporation, Dayton Newspapers, Inc., NCR, and TRW. In 1984 Xavier University of Cincinnati joined, and the consortium was renamed the Southern Ohio Consortium of Colleges and Universities.

The stated purposes of the organization were to promote cooperative beneficial interaction among the institutions and to build a link between local colleges and universities and businesses and industries for area economic development. For a variety of reasons, the first objective succeeded while the second failed.

In the meantime the decay of downtown Springfield became increasingly apparent. While Springfield wondered if Rike's from Dayton or Lazarus from Columbus would build a store in Springfield, the stores already there closed in large numbers. Empty or unrepaired storefronts were becoming more visible by the mid-1950s. By 1960 the decline of the downtown area was a frequent topic of conversation.

A major factor in downtown decay was the automobile. America's love for the auto and the absence of parking space in the downtown area led to zoning revisions and the development of small shopping centers in Springfield—Park Shopping Center at First Street and Bechtle Avenue in 1955, and Southern Village on Selma Road were just the first. In addition Springfielders and residents of the county drove to Dayton, Columbus, and even Cincinnati in ever-increasing numbers to avail themselves of more stores, larger stores, and greater selection.

Eventually out-of-town developers built Upper Valley Mall in the Mad River flood plain, paving over the beautiful fields that had been drained just thirty years before. The mall housed eighty-one stores, most from out of town. It also attracted a number of stores from downtown Springfield and caused other downtown stores to close. Soon, for several miles in either direction, a countryside shopping area developed that attracted not only Springfield and Clark County residents, but shoppers from surrounding counties.

The Springfield-Clark County area was also affected by national and international developments. The tensions of the Cold War, the Korean and Vietnamese conflicts, and the ongoing concern for nuclear war had their impact on the area. Young people in particular were caught up in the massive popular turmoil of the Vietnam War. Student unrest at colleges and universities and the growth of protest music and protest behavior affected schools in Springfield and the surrounding community.

The radical movement of student power, black unrest, and youth alienation of the late 1960s and early 1970s troubled area residents. The unpopular Vietnam War, with the dissent surrounding it; a growing concern about the economy; the excesses of youth peer culture in drugs, sex, and rock music; the breakdown of student responsibility; and the assault on parental authority had less impact in Springfield than elsewhere, but they were not without influence.

Nowhere was the tension more evident than in race relations. The new black residents from Appalachia and other blacks found life together in Springfield uncomfortable. Local blacks, encouraged by the national Civil Rights movement and finding support among the white population, pushed to achieve a greater realization of their rights in Springfield. The roots of the local movement were deep. Hattie Mosely, a black insurance saleswoman, had helped organize the Civil Rights Protective League in Springfield in the 1920s. A protégée, Dorothy Bacon, captured the spirit of the Springfield black community in the 1950s, and in the 1960s tied the Springfield movement to the national cause. A local chapter of the National Association for the Advancement of Colored People (NAACP) was established, and Dorothy Bacon was elected secretary. Early in the 1960s civil rights leader Medgar Evers came from Mississippi to speak in Springfield at an NAACP meeting in the Wiley Methodist Church.

During these years blacks in Springfield staged sit-ins at the Liberty Theater, which refused to sell tickets to blacks, and supported efforts to compel merchants to treat customers equally. They opposed de facto segregation in area schools and charged that the system essentially provided separate and unequal schools because of segregated

neighborhoods and discrimination in real estate and mortgage transactions.

As early as the 1950s a black man sought to run for city commission, but he was disqualified on the grounds that his petitions did not have enough signatures of registered voters. Efforts were made thereafter to get more blacks registered to vote. In 1961 Robert C. Henry became the first black person elected to the Springfield City Commission and the first to serve at that level of government in the town's history. Four years later Henry received more votes than any other candidate, and his fellow commissioners elected him mayor of Springfield in 1966. Henry was the first black man in America to serve as mayor in a city of Springfield's size or larger.

Henry succeeded Maurice K. "Buddy" Baach, the city's first Jewish mayor, who had served from 1964 to 1965. In his two terms as mayor, his administration extended sewer lines north to the new International Harvester plant site, acquired George Rogers Clark Park as a city park, developed Reid Park, and opened the city's first public swimming pool on North Bechtle Avenue.

The community made real progress in meeting some local needs. In 1958 the city dedicated its new and completely modern waterworks on Eagle City Road north of town. A succession of city commissioners worked successfully on plans and proposals for the reconstruction of downtown sewers, particularly Mill Run, a prerequisite to any downtown renewal. Community leaders also worked to develop the Springfield Municipal Airport south of town. In 1966 International Harvester completed a new truck plant north of Springfield, indicating a major commitment to production expansion.

There was renewed progress in the arts. In 1958 the Youth Symphony was organized. In 1962 the Civic Opera held its first season. By 1967 Jackson Wiley, conductor of the Springfield Symphony since 1957 and a member of the music faculty at Wittenberg, established the Springfield Summer Arts Festival, out of which grew the Springfield Arts Council. The Springfield Art Center was also built in 1967. The building of schools began in the 1950s as a response to the baby boom. A new North High School was completed in 1960. The joint city-county vocational school was opened in 1967 by Springfield native Richard O. Brinkman. In 1966 the state chartered the first technical institute in Ohio history, and Brinkman was selected as the first president of Clark Technical College,

Opposite
John F. Kennedy visited Springfield during his 1960 presidential campaign. Kennedy is pictured surrounded by a cheering crowd as his motorcade entered the Wittenberg University football field. Seated beside him in the car is Ohio Governor Michael V. Disalle. From the Wittenberg University Archives

which opened in 1968.

In 1966 the first clearcut move toward downtown revitalization was undertaken. Howard B. Noonan, chairman of the board of the Kissell Company, (one of the nation's largest real estate mortgage companies) called a meeting of citizens to form the Community Action Now (CAN) Committee. The name was chosen to promote a "we can" attitude in the community to overcome the psychological depression caused by the Crowell closing and the demoralization of the ensuing decade. Original members of the group were Howard Noonan, chairman; Peter Dennerlein, former plant manager at Crowell's; local industrialists Edward Coleman, Joseph Shouvlin, and Alvin McGregor; attorneys Bitner Browne and Robert Acton; Pastor Kay Glaesner; President John Stauffer of Wittenberg; newspaper publisher Robert Hamilton; area industrialists Reed Robertson and H.D. Crabtree; Bob Yontz, owner of radio station WBLY; and *The Springfield Daily News* editor Loren Schultz.

However, in 1967 opponents of renewal and taxation secured passage of three charter amendments restricting the city's fair-housing powers and the commissioner's urban-renewal powers. These moves blocked the community from access to federally funded programs to assist in revitalizing the downtown area or old neighborhoods. The efforts of the CAN Committee were thus effectively stymied.

Springfielders voted down a city income tax increase in 1968 which was designed to further downtown renewal. On that unlikely election day, a new city manager, Al Strozdas, arrived. His calm and astute leadership of community government would build confidence and lead to greater community success.

In 1969 a Committee of Twenty-One, composed of local labor, business, and institutional leaders, was organized to seek ways to finance downtown improvements and to support the new city manager. Chaired by the Reverend Kenneth P. Murphy, pastor of the United Church of Christ, the group sought funding for a new city hall and redevelopment of the center block downtown. Labor leaders Frank P. Burns of the Plumbers Local 97 and Howard W. Carder of the Carpenters and Joiners Union Local 660 took the initiative in securing the repeal of the 1967 amendment preventing downtown renewal. They formed a committee of Burns, Carder, Howard Noonan, H.D. Crabtree, local labor leader Clell Boggs, industrialists Harold Karr, Edward Carter, and Robert Horstman, and several business leaders. It was an impressive group. Sherwood Moran was selected to direct this successful labor-management campaign to repeal Section 90 of the city charter, clearing the way for city renewal action.

During 1971 black City Commissioner Robert L. Burton revealed plans for a new city building. Burton also called

for the revitalization of the entire business district with a shopping mall, a city-county government center, a parking garage, and a metropolitan housing project. The Springfield Chamber of Commerce revealed a downtown development plan calling for a multi-story city-county administration building, a safety building to house the jail, the police, and the Clark County sheriff, and a building for area courts—municipal, common pleas, and probate.

To bring the Burton and Chamber of Commerce ideas together and to coordinate city and county plans for area development, Howard Noonan organized the Blueprint for Progress Committee to act as a coordinating body. Members included Noonan, labor leader Frank Burns, City Mayor Robert Burton, Edward Carter, businesswoman Jody Gatten, financier Paul Hellmuth, county commissioner Carl Mumma, merchant Edward Munley, publisher of *The Springfield News and Sun* Robert Hamilton, city commissioner Robert Pyle, and *The Springfield Daily News* editor Loren Schultz.

In 1972 voters in Clark County passed a "piggyback" sales tax, adding a half-percent local tax to the state rate. The funds were not directed toward all the projects being discussed by the Blueprint for Progress Committee, but toward a new juvenile center and a city-county safety building.

To better organize to stimulate downtown development, local business leaders formed the Core Renewal Corporation. In the new structure, city and county would not be active participants, but the corporation could contract with either one or both government bodies. Paul Hellmuth was chairman of the board of directors, realtor Martin Levine was president, Howard Noonan and Peter Noonan were vice-presidents, Andrew Hellmuth was secretary, and Thomas Loftis was treasurer. Core Renewal Corporation developed plans for the city to initiate downtown renewal.

All such plans came face to face with a growing fundamental problem: the city and county tax bases were going through a transition. The city's tax base was shrinking as old industries moved, and the county's tax base was growing as new developments like the International Harvester plant and Upper Valley Mall were constructed outside city limits. City development would increasingly require a

growing rate of taxation on a shrinking tax base, unless mutual city-county planning took place.

The Committee of Twenty-One, after several years of inactivity, was revived to discuss funding possibilities. It recommended increasing the city income tax to fund a new city building. Robert Ashbaugh of the United Auto Workers (UAW), and Robert Benston of the AFL-CIO, along with Fred Leventhal, co-owner of the Vining Broom Company, and Jody Gatten, submitted a program for financing that the committee and the city commission approved for a June 3, 1975, election—Issues 7 and 6.

"Citizens for a Better Springfield," chaired by Fred Leventhal, with Jody Gatten as campaign director, pushed for passage of Issues 7 and 6 as Springfield prepared to celebrate the nation's bicentennial in 1976. The issues passed, and downtown revitalization moved forward. The Core Renewal Corporation began the purchase and demolition of property in the core block (bounded on the north by Main Street, on the west by Fountain Avenue, on the south by High Street, and on the east by Limestone Street) on behalf of the city under the Impacted Cities Act passed by the state legislature.

The first building to be erected in the core was a new city building, and in 1977 the new city hall was dedicated. It was planned that the earliest construction downtown would be by the government, but that private capital would be encouraged to add to the development. In 1980 the new City-County Safety Building was constructed. First among private downtown construction was the Springfield Bank with a new building at Main Street and Fountain Avenue.

Next, Credit Life Insurance Company and Security National Bank erected buildings across from one another at High and Limestone streets. Bob Hollenbeck and Wesley Harrison of Credit Life and Security National Bank made major commitments to downtown renewal that kept the project moving. Leaders of the Merchants and Mechanics Federal Savings and Loan Association joined in the private sector efforts with the decision to build the new M & M building at Main and Limestone streets.

Within a few years Credit Life sold its new building to Clark Technical College for a downtown center and built a new ten-story Credit Life Building at Main and Limestone streets in the core block. The Merchants and Mechanics Federal Savings and Loan Association built its new building at the corner of Main and Limestone. By the early 1980s plans were in place to renovate and restore the 100-year-old Arcade Building and the old city building for shops, theaters, and restaurants.

The whole downtown project was first delayed by opponents of taxation and urban renewal. It was then stymied by city-county conflict and disagreement. It was finally virtually halted altogether by high interest rates

Opposite, left
In 1966 Robert C. Henry became the first black man in America to serve as mayor in a city of Springfield's size or larger. First elected to the city commission in 1961, Henry later received more votes than any other candidate when he was reelected in 1965. Courtesy, Springfield Newspapers, Inc.

Opposite, right
Maurice K. "Buddy" Bach became Springfield's first Jewish mayor in 1964. Courtesy, Springfield Newspapers, Inc.

Opposite
Downtown, once thronging with people, began to look deserted in the early 1960s as stores became vacant and empty windows lined the sidewalks. In 1966 the CAN commitee made the first move toward downtown revitalization. Courtesy, City of Springfield

Right
Reconstruction of the city's sewer system was essential to downtown renewal. Workers in Mill Run are pictured about 1975. Courtesy, City of Springfield

and the recessions of 1974 to 1976 and 1979 to 1982. The persistence of downtown developers and the commitment of local business leaders, in spite of such problems, reflected the city's determination to overcome its troubles and to thrive.

Determination and resolve were tested once again in the struggle of International Harvester to survive as a company. In 1976 the Springfield plant celebrated the production of the one millionth truck at the new plant. The year 1979 had been the best year ever at IH. The company earned $469 million on sales of $8.4 billion. By 1982 sales had been cut nearly in half to $4.2 billion. The company lost $1.6 billion and faced bankruptcy. A combination of problems caused the rapid turn of events. The company had become locked in a major strike with the UAW, each side determined not to give in. Labor recalled years of record profits, management saw the need to compete in a new and tougher world market. International Harvester Chairman and President Archie McArdle seemed intent upon changing the balance of power in the company's relationship with the union—to destroy it, according to union leadership—and a settlement seemed impossible.

In the midst of the six-month strike the nation's and the world's economy slipped into recession. Backlogged orders for trucks vanished. When settlement of the strike came, business was so bad that mass layoffs were inevitable. The company became involved in a struggle to stay afloat with massive loans from banks. Archie McArdle was replaced by Donald D. Lennox, who set about redesigning and restructuring and, it was hoped, saving the company. The nation's leading manufacturer of heavy- and medium-duty trucks and number two maker of agricultural equipment was in deep trouble. Its plants, with the exception of the one in Springfield, were outdated, markets and sales had shriveled, and its debts passed four billion dollars.

Lennox sold off seventeen operations and cut head count and payroll by one-third. In the process, the company deliberated on whether to consolidate its U.S. truck manufacturing in Springfield or Fort Wayne. The losing plant would be closed. A group of Springfield citizens went to work to influence the IH decision. Included in

the group were Dennis Shere, publisher of *The Springfield News-Sun;* Richard L. Kuss of Bonded Oil; Larry Krukewitt of the Springfield Chamber of Commerce; Donald L. Bishop, retired banker and development consultant with Wittenberg University; and Martin Levine, local realtor and developer. If the IH plant in Springfield could not be saved, and that was the primary objective, the group at least wanted to avoid a repeat of the fate of the local Crowell-Collier plant in 1956. If the IH plant was not going to continue, it should not sit empty for a period of years. Such an outcome would be disastrous.

The group put together a package for a $27.6 million purchase-lease-back agreement, $9.2 million to come from the Ohio Department of Economic and Community Development and $18.4 million from eleven area banks and savings and loan associations. They also secured a state guarantee of eighty-five percent of the bank loan. The financing was provided through the Commmunity Improvement Corporation of Springfield and Clark County (CIC). The Community Improvement Corporation was the old Industrial Development Division of the Springfield Chamber of Commerce, reorganized and redesigned to conform to legislation designed to promote community development through the joint efforts of government and private enterprise. Fort Wayne's leadership put together a package of more than thirty million dollars. The assistance packages were nearly equal. Under the Springfield plan, if IH should fail the plant would become the property of the local CIC, and the city could market it immediately to another truck maker.

The decision, made on September 27, 1982, was to locate in Springfield. It was favored for many reasons: its more modern facility, lower energy consumption, automated high-rise warehouse, efficient material delivery system, and high-volume capability. A real plus was the generosity of the CIC funding package.

Production capacity at the Springfield plant was scheduled to increase, and about 1,500 new jobs would eventually be created. The stakes were high for both cities—each could lose its major employer or gain 1,500 jobs. The tug-of-war lasted for sixty days before the announcement that eventually favored Springfield was made.

The good news about International Harvester came back-to-back with the good news of success in the financial campaign for Wittenberg. In 1979 Wittenberg had begun a national campaign for $16.7 million. In November 1982 national campaign chairman Richard L. Kuss announced that more than twenty million dollars had been committed in three years. A new library and a new health, physical education, and recreation center were the two most visible benefits.

The school's reputation grew, and it appeared on several listings of the top 250 schools in the nation. In November 1983 *U.S. News & World Report* listed Wittenberg as one of the seven best smaller, comprehensive institutions east of the Mississippi in a special feature entitled "Ranking the Colleges." The story placed Wittenberg among a select top five percent of American colleges and universities.

Springfield and Clark County enjoyed media attention as well. The coverage of the decision of IH and Wittenberg's growing reputation reflected well on the city and county. In addition the Wittenberg Tigers football team garnered national television exposure for the school and the community as Division III college ball replaced the professionals during the National Football League strike.

In 1983 *Newsweek* selected Springfield and Clark County as the focus of its 50th-anniversary issue, tracing the impact of the events of half a century on five families in a typical American community. The magazine hailed Springfield and Clark County as "the American dream."

Yet Springfield's past glory, according to turn-of-the-century observer W.F. Austin, came by overcoming disadvantages. The area was always poor in natural resources, but rich in people "against whom misfortune and failure seemed powerless."

In 1984 Mayor Leland Schuler, area Chamber of Commerce chairman James Foreman, and others worked with city, county, and township leaders to revive that spirit and to develop an area agenda that would include economic development as its basis.

The establishment of industrial parks that would be fully serviced with city utilities and which would help the city tax base were an important part of their thinking.

After many weeks of negotiation, several such sites were on the way to reality, and area confidence grew.

Another element in the emerging agenda was a rededication to renewal of the downtown core of the city. The Market Square renovation project, converting the turn-of-the-century City Building to modern commercial space, moved toward completion. The farmer's market on the ground floor was restored and reopened. The plan for the upper floors included a restaurant and restoration of the old city auditorium as a theater. Following the Market Square project were plans for the restoration of the Arcade Hotel as a modern retail space.

This persevering community has been the birthplace and/or home of a host of inventors, industrialists, entrepreneurs, and scientists, whose contributions have been chronicled in Springfield and Clark County's history. It has also been the hometown of artists such as Worthington Whitridge, Godfrey Frankenstein, Jerome Uhl, Walter Tittle, Frank Myers Boggs, Roy McAdams, E.C. Bradshaw, Ralston Thompson, and John Schlump. Authors have been nurtured here, including Marion Lewis Renick, Sherwood Anderson, Lloyd C. Douglas, Samuel Shellabarger, Isaac K. Funk and Adam W. Wagnalls, John H.W. Stuckenberg, and Samuel McChord Crothers.

Nationally-known entertainers such as showman Gus Sun, Lillian and Dorothy Gish, Sybal Fagan, and Jonathan Winters spent the young years of their lives in Springfield. Sports figures including prizefighter Davey Moore, baseball player Brooks Lawrence, and pitcher Harvey Haddix represent the best of the community's strong athletic heritage.

Together these individuals attest to the area's rich tradition in talent and human development. All were influenced by the local people and atmosphere. What is ahead for Springfield and Clark County? The answer rests with its citizens, as it always has before, and with those who will emerge to give form and direction to people's hopes and aspirations.

The community's agenda for the future is becoming clear: striving for improved confidence in city and county government; placing a greater focus on neighborhood developments; planning for commercial, industrial, and urban growth in both city and county; and giving stronger attention to the quality of life provided for all citizens by its schools, libraries, parks, and other social and cultural opportunities. The people of Springfield and Clark County are up to the challenge.

Opposite
Springfield's new City Building was dedicated in 1979. Courtesy, City of Springfield

8 *Partners in Progress*

First, there was the wilderness. There was incredible rich and rolling land ... loam, towered over by sixty-foot trees, and thick, human-defying poison ivy and honeysuckle growing so profusely that, with their natural compatriots, they ruled the wilderness that is now Springfield and Clark County, Ohio.

Into this fantastic natural wilderness, plowing through the young scrub oak and the hawthorn, walking tall beneath the willows and the dogwood and the redbud, came the Indians. They were followed later by white settlers.

The arrival of settlers brought changes to the wilderness. By 1749 the buffalo were almost gone; the panthers disappeared by 1830; and the ruddy duck, a native delicacy, was gone by about 1870. And, of course, the plant life in the wilderness was itself cleared away to make room for homes and roads.

Against this background and, indeed, within it, humans played out their games of survival and conquest. They eventually tamed the wilderness to suit their purposes.

Once the wilderness began to be controlled, and the Indians were subdued, human settlers in this area began to increase rapidly; in order to thrive as well as simply survive, they added commerce and trade to the other changes occurring in the vast wilderness.

Businesses have come and gone in Springfield and Clark County since the establishment of the first white settlement in the early years of the nineteenth century in New Boston. Large operations, small family-owned and -operated enterprises, and businesses that are part of larger worldwide conglomerates have been and are a part of area business, industry, education, service, and religious organizations.

The enterprises whose stories are detailed on the following pages have chosen to support this important literary and civic project. They illustrate the variety of ways in which individuals and their businesses have contributed to the area's growth and development. The civic involvement of Springfield's businesses, institutions of learning, and local government, in cooperation with its citizens, has made the community an excellent place to live and work.

Opposite
Trans World Airline's Star of Springfield *inaugurated regularly scheduled commercial service at Springfield Airport on the morning of March 1, 1948. Carl Berg (left) of the Chamber of Commerce and Oscar Fleckner, city manager, presided at the ceremonies. The flight originated in New York, made nine other stops, and arrived in Los Angeles twenty-one hours later. Courtesy, Springfield Newspapers, Inc.*

CLARK COUNTY HISTORICAL SOCIETY

One of the oldest cultural institutions in Springfield, the Clark County Historical Society, was incorporated on October 4, 1897. Such prominent citizens as P.O. Mast, Thomas F. McGrew, Ira W. Wallace, Oscar T. Martin, F.M. Hagen, Theo Troupe, H.S. Showers, John M. Smally, Oran F. Hypes, and A.F. Linn were the charter members.

The institution's founding was inspired by the advance preparations for celebrating the centennial of Springfield's settlement in 1901. In 1880 many of the society's charter members had worked for or participated in the activities commemorating the centennial of the Battle of Piqua at George Rogers Clark Park.

From its modest beginnings the society grew quickly and soon occupied its first home in rooms in the former Municipal Court Building (now County Building No. 3) on the southeast corner of Limestone and Columbia streets.

Here, through generous donations from local citizens, the society began building its collection of county artifacts, which today number more than 150,000, in its principal museum on the upper floors of Memorial Hall at 300 West Main Street. A 2,000-volume library, Clark County records, and bound volumes of local newspapers in "rag" form are among the artifacts stored and exhibited at Memorial Hall.

In addition to this museum, the society has concentrated on restoring the David Crabill Homestead, its out-

The David Crabill Homestead at C.J. Brown Dam and Reservoir is the Clark County Historical Society's outdoor interpretive museum.

door interpretive museum that overlooks Clarence J. Brown Reservoir. Farm implements from the nineteenth century are arranged there to illustrate the life of Ohio pioneers in the 1830s.

The society's annex, located at the Clark County Fairgrounds at State Route 41 and Interstate 70, east of Springfield, houses oversized collections, including farm machinery, a Conestoga wagon, and carriages. Emmanuel Church, a one-story structure built in 1856, was also renovated by volunteers as a fourth museum for the society.

During Springfield's centennial

A gallery of the Clark County Historical Society's principal museum, located on the upper floors of Memorial Hall, as it appeared during the 1984 Christmas season.

year, the society accepted a one-acre parcel of land that later became the nucleus of George Rogers Clark Park, which has been a state, then city, and now a county park. It is located west of the city limits off State Route 4. By 1924 the society had promoted the erection of a statue of General Clark on that site.

The society has always been active in efforts to preserve such historical structures as the old City Building on the Esplanade. In the past four decades it has pursued an active publishing program, with many of its publications being written by scholars within Clark County.

Its publications include Mary A. Skardon's *The Attack on Fort Liberty and the Battle of Piqua,* David R. Collins' *Archaeology of Clark County,* William A. Kinnison and Mary A. Skardon's *World War I 50th Anniversary 1918-1968,* and Willard D. Allbeck's *Springfield in the 1870s.*

With more than 700 members today, the Clark County Historical Society is preparing to mark its 200th anniversary in slightly more than a decade. It currently works actively with more than twenty local historical groups to help preserve the county's history. The society looks to the future as it attempts to preserve the past. Its plans include a major museum, additional publications, and more intense educational publication efforts.

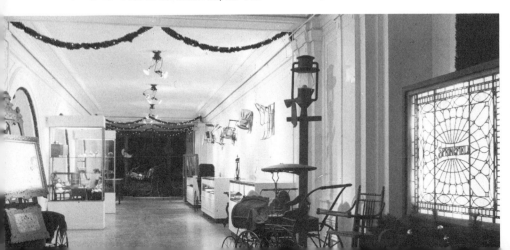

WITTENBERG UNIVERSITY

Wittenberg University was founded in Springfield because descendants of early German Lutheran immigrants who had settled in Ohio felt a need for an institution to train preachers in English for Ohio and the West.

A fully accredited, residential, undergraduate, liberal arts university committed to academic excellence and the development of the individual, Wittenberg, in 1983, was rated one of the nation's highest-quality undergraduate schools by college presidents.

As with many institutions, Wittenberg's history and its relationship with the city and county in which it is located have been shaped by the interests and personalities of its presidents.

Ezra Keller, although he was not officially inaugurated as president until 1847, heavily influenced the selection of Springfield as Wittenberg's site in 1845, the year in which classes began. He felt that the National Road from Maryland would be the gateway to the West for thousands.

The tone of Wittenberg as a Christian, liberal arts college was set by its second president, Samuel Sprecher.

John B. Helwig's administration was one of strife and change. During his tenure, the board of directors reaffirmed an open admissions policy for all races and approved the admission of women to the college.

Significant changes in the educational program were announced in the 1883 catalog during Samuel Alfred Ort's presidency. A scientific course and a literary course joined the classical bachelor of arts course in the curriculum. Later, during Ort's presidency, the Wittenberg College Conservatory of Music emerged, exerting a positive influence on music in Springfield, allowing city and college musical efforts to reinforce one another.

President John M. Ruthrauff died unexpectedly in the second year of

Recitation Hall, Wittenberg's current administrative building, as it appeared in 1886 when it housed classrooms.

his administration. His successor, Charles Girven Heckert, was the first faculty member to be named the college's president. He brought a focus on faculty strength and academic excellence to the institution.

Dr. Rees Edgar Tulloss was president during a time of unprecedented expansion in American higher education. Extracurricular activities thrived; theater, debate, athletics, music, and the Greek system all grew. Dr. Tulloss' 29-year administration, which ended in 1949, spanned the Roaring Twenties, the Great Depression, and World War II.

Growth from fourteen to thirty campus buildings, from an enrollment of 917 to 1,886 students, and from assets of $5,922,228 to $23,700,000 occurred during the fourteen years that Clarence Charles Stoughton was president. Under Stoughton's leadership, the first Annual Alumni Fund was conducted in 1950. More than one million dollars was raised through these funds for faculty salaries and student aid during his administration. Dr. Stoughton broadened the base of Lutheran church support and attracted increased resources from the community. "College" was dropped from the

Myers Hall, one of the university's original buildings, sits atop the highest hill on campus.

school's title when it became Wittenberg University on September 1, 1959.

Subsequent presidents inherited a vigorous and prosperous institution of wide reputation and solid strength from Stoughton. Dr. John N. Stauffer, who had been dean since 1957, was president from 1963 to 1968. His successor, Dr. G. Kenneth Andeen, the first ordained president since Tulloss, served until 1970. Wittenberg's eleventh and current president, William A. Kinnison, an educator, administrator, and historian, is the university's first Springfield-born president.

SPECO DIVISION, KELSEY-HAYES COMPANY

In 1908 J.E. McAdams opened the doors to the Gem City Machine Company, in Dayton, to manufacture tools, dies, jigs, and fixtures.

Six years later McAdams opened the Springfield branch of his Dayton firm in a building on Park Street (now Dakota Avenue) north of West Columbia Street, and named it Steel Products Engineering Company. In about 1885 this building had been occupied by the Tricycle Shop for the manufacture of tricycles and boys' wagons. The Springfield Gas Engine Company moved its operation to this location from Washington Street in 1904 and the

manufacture of tricycles ceased.

McAdams had sold the Dayton plant and consolidated all activities in Springfield by 1923. He remained president and owner of the firm until it was acquired in 1955 by Kelsey-Hayes, at which time it became the SPECO Division, currently located northwest of Springfield on Baker Road. In 1973, Kelsey-Hayes became a wholly owned subsidiary of the Fruehauf Corporation. The original three-story plant at 1205 West Columbia Street was completely destroyed by fire in August 1984.

Lawrence E. Rausenberger joined Steel Products Engineering dur-

ing the pre-World War I period. The firm designed and developed Rausenberger's twelve-cylinder, V-type aircraft engine, which developed 160 horsepower at 320 rpm. Rausenberger, who was chief aeronautical engineer from 1926 until 1950, developed the engine in the first airplane that flew over the Andes Mountains. He knew the Wright brothers personally, and an engine that he developed is now on display in their airplane, *The Flyer,* at the Air Force Museum in Dayton.

During World War I the company became the first private contractor to manufacture four-inch naval gun

Original plant—Steel Products Engineering Company, 1205 West Columbia Street.

sights. Prior to this time, all sights had been produced at the Naval Gun Factory in Washington, D.C.

Steel Products Engineering became involved in the overhaul of the Liberty aircraft engine in 1918. The work on the Liberty engines, and the redesigning of them into inverted-type engines for more advanced aircraft, continued into the 1920s.

Meanwhile, the plans and designs for a new engine developed by Rausenberger in 1918 led to a contract with McCook Field (now Wright-Patterson Air Force Base) in Dayton in 1920. The Rausie E-6 upright, six-cylinder, water-cooled verti-cal-line engine, which could reach 175 horsepower at 1,650 rpm, was delivered in April 1921, and proved to be a great success. In fifty hours of government testing, the Rausie E-6 broke several records, including less gas and oil consumption. The Rausie E-6 weighed 550 pounds, or 3.14 pounds per horsepower. Even after being run for an hour beyond the normal test time, no appreciable wear was found on the engine.

Charles Brehm perfected the Brehm trimming idea for Steel Prod-ucts Engineering in 1923. In the metal-fabricating industry, it became known as the "Shimmy Die." This die trimmed round, square, angular, and irregular-shaped shells drawn from sheet metal varying in size from a woman's small watch case to a refrigerator door.

Also in 1923 the company designed, developed, and prototyped the Morehouse engine for the first lighter-than-air aircraft in the United States. This was a two-cylinder, four-cycle air-cooled, flat-type engine. The Morehouse engine was first used to furnish an air ballast for a dirigible.

The Rausie H-6 engine was developed in 1929. It developed 135 horsepower at 3,400 rpm. It was a six-cylinder, vertical-line, air-cooled aircraft engine. That same year, SPE designed and developed a four-cylinder, 100 horsepower, inverted straight air-cooled aircraft engine for the Reinhart-Whelan Company of Dayton.

During the years between World Wars I and II, the firm also designed and developed tools, dies, fixtures, and special machinery for nonmilitary customers, including the National Biscuit Company's machine that made bite-size shredded wheat cereal, the Averback Shaper, and Procter and Gamble's Crisco blending machine.

SPE designed and developed a six-cylinder, water-cooled automobile engine for the A. L. Powell Company in 1930. In the mid-1930s, under the guidance of Lawrence Rausenberger, the firm designed and developed the Rausie GV-600, twelve-cylinder, inverted V-type engine for the U.S. Navy. This air-cooled engine rated 3,850 rpm at 450 horsepower, which was said to be the highest rpm on an aircraft engine in the United States at that time.

As World War II approached, SPE helped develop the first counter-rotation aircraft propeller with hydraulic pitch control, and, with Sperry Gyroscope Company, began working on the first aircraft machine-gun turret to be manufactured in this country.

More production space was required as World War II spread throughout Europe. So the firm bought the Mast-Foos Company building across Dakota Avenue, and, with the permission of the city, sealed off the street and joined its original building with its new purchase. In addition, SPE bought the Cincinnati and Lake Erie Traction Company's car barn on West North Street and dubbed it Plant No. 2.

Continuing its cooperation with the Sperry Gyroscope Company, Steel Products Engineering designed and produced the upper and lower gun turrets for the Boeing B-17 Bomber. The top gun turret was manually operated while the lower one was remotely controlled from a central sighting system. Several thousand of the top gun turrets were produced for the B-17.

During World War II the firm helped develop and produce variable pitch propeller hubs for the Curtis Wright Company.

The dedicated efforts of Steel Products Engineering employees were rewarded by the federal government on July 28, 1944, when Army Brigadier General Orval R. Cook presented McAdams with the coveted Army/Navy "E" flag, an award for excellence and efficiency in production. More than 3,000 people attended the ceremony when the flag was presented. Navy Captain J. Ross Allen presented an "E" lapel pin to six people representing all employees: J.M. Payne, president of the Association of Steel Products Engineering Company Employees; Mrs. Dorothy Barr Gothard, a Gold Star Mother; Ralph Calhoun, oldest employee; Earl E. Kirkwood, the first employee in Plant No. 2; Leroy D. Carpenter, an honorably discharged veteran of the war; and Mrs. Lulu Fay Shaw, the first female employee. Later all em-

ployees received an 'E' lapel pin.

General Cook said, "In the splendid turrets, delivered by the thousands, you have contributed to the magnificent records of our Flying Fortresses times without number. ... As changes in tactics and equipment demanded technical changes and improvements, without failing in your production schedule, you collaborated in the redesign and engineering work that brought about these improvements."

The Patterson Field Color Guard and the 661st Air Force Band participated in the ceremony, which was emceed by William "Big Bill" Jordan, vice-president and general manager.

Between the end of World War II and the Korean War, the company's major development projects included experimental engines, helicopter

transmissions, gun turrets, and bomb hoists.

Built to U.S. Air Force design, gun turrets for the B-36 Bomber were also manufactured by Steel Products Engineering. Additional work for the Air Force included the design of a seventeen-ton hydraulic aircraft jack in 1946, the development of a thirty-caliber gun mount for a Marine Corps tank, and the design and development of a C-9 bomb hoist in 1947. SPECO later produced quantities of C-5 and K-4 bomb hoists for the B-52 Bomber.

In the late 1940s Steel Products Engineering helped pioneer the development of helicopter transmissions, which transfer the power from the high-speed engine or turbine to the helicopter rotor blades. Transmissions for the Bell Helicopter

Present plant—SPECO Division, Kelsey-Hayes Company, 2941 Baker Road.

Company Model 47 Helicopter were produced in quantity. These helicopters were used in Korea and were the type widely seen on the television series, "M.A.S.H."

Subsequent programs included the quantity production of transmissions for the Bell HU-1 "Huey" Helicopter, which was later used by the thousands in Vietnam, and the Piasecki Helicopter Company (now the Boeing-Vertol Company) H-21 "Flying Banana."

While the United States was involved in the Korean War, the firm expanded its product line to include rotating radar antenna mounts. Nearly 1,000 mounts were produced under contracts to the Bell Telephone Laboratories and the Western Electric Company for the M-33 antiaircraft gunfire director. In 1951 Steel

Products Engineering designed, developed, and manufactured for these same companies significant quantities of tracking and guidance antenna mounts for their Nike-Hercules antiaircraft missile systems.

Later products included WS-107A Antenna Mounts for guiding the early Air Force "Titan" intercontinental ballistic missile; the AN/MSG-3 Marine Corps land-based "Terrier" missile; the Raytheon Company's "Hawk" missile; and the Bell Aerospace Company's SPN-10 Automatic Landing System for aircraft carriers.

SPECO also designed and developed the prototype tracking and

guidance antenna mounts for the Army's Nike-Zeus antimissile system to be used to destroy incoming ICBMs. This was said to be like trying to "hit a bullet with a bullet." At the time, these antenna mounts were probably the most accurate in the world. This mechanical product line was technically eliminated by an electronic phase array antenna system, which is fixed and does not rotate.

In 1956 SPECO purchased sixty-eight acres of land on Baker Road, a site that is now its only home. Since the Korean War, the firm has concentrated on the markets for helicopter transmissions, aircraft actuation systems, power drives, and accessory gearboxes.

Quantity transmission production has been achieved for the commercial Bell 206 Jet Ranger Helicopter and the Sikorsky Company's Military H-60 "Black Hawk" series, which is today's U.S. Army utility helicopter.

Wing-flap actuators are the muscles that extend and retract the flaps on the leading and trailing edges of an aircraft wing. Since 1958 SPECO has produced such systems for transport, surveillance, or bomber-type aircraft made by Lockheed (models P-3, C-141, C-5); Grumman (models G-1, E-2C, C-2A); and Rockwell International (Model B-1). Of particular interest is the flap-actuation system used on the C-5 series aircraft, the world's largest airplane.

In the mid-1970s SPECO designed and built the complex tilt rotor-actuation system for the Bell XV-15 experimental aircraft.

Continuing to design and manufacture precision-machined devices for aircraft power transmission and flight controls, employees of the SPECO Division, Kelsey-Hayes Company, today take the same pride in excellence and efficiency that marked their predecessors who were so highly honored by the presentation of the Army/Navy "E" flag in 1944.

CLARK TECHNICAL COLLEGE

Clark Technical College is a name now widely known in and beyond Clark County. But, because it was so new and different in 1965, the Ohio Board of Regents denied the request for a college charter for the three-year-old Springfield and Clark County Technical Education Program. However, on February 18, 1966, the regents did charter the Clark County Technical Institute, which was the first technical institute chartered in Ohio.

In 1962 the new school's seventy-eight students, ages ranging from eighteen to forty-two, were housed in a wing of Springfield North High School. Clark Technical College currently enrolls 2,700 students and has awarded more than 4,500 associate degrees and certificates.

Clark's initial success was largely

The Leffel Lane Campus of Clark Technical College.

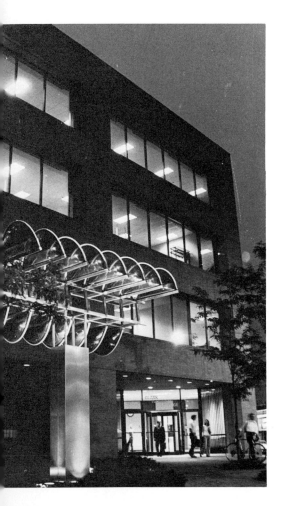

Clark Technical College's Brinkman Education Center, at High and Limestone streets in downtown Springfield, opened its doors in 1981.

the result of the efforts of Richard O. Brinkman, its first president, a committed board of trustees, and a small group of dedicated staff. Brinkman retired in June 1983 following the college's twenty-first commencement.

Clark benefitted from the national emphasis on science and technology that followed *Sputnik* in the late 1950s and also from Ohio's movement during the 1960s to put college opportunities within reach for every citizen. At the sixty-acre Leffel Lane Campus, construction began in 1967 on buildings that became Rhodes Hall and Shull Hall. The Library Resource Center was opened in 1972, followed by the Applied Science Center in 1975. These facilities virtually completed a campus that is a sparkling asset to the community as well as to the college. The Brinkman Center, part of a community emphasis on economic revitalization,

opened its doors in downtown Springfield in 1981 and now houses business technology programs, college-wide computer facilities, and a superb conference center for community services.

By 1972 the name of the institution had been changed to Clark Technical College and initial programs in mechanical and electrical engineering technologies and data processing had been expanded to include courses of study in agriculture, business, health, and public-service technologies.

Today Clark continues efforts to provide college opportunity and community service on an ever-broadening range of workshops, short courses, and degree programs. The role of the college in the changing economy of the community, including education and manpower needs, is constantly evolving, but unchanged in its essence: higher-education opportunity with excellence.

Clark Technical College welcomed its second president, Dr. George H. Robertson, in 1983. The institution continues to educate and guide each individual student toward his or her maximum physical, intellectual, and moral potential.

M&M FEDERAL SAVINGS AND LOAN ASSOCIATION

President E.C. Gwynn announced that the Merchants and Mechanics Building and Loan Company would open for business on February 25, 1892, in an upstairs room of the Zimmerman Building, located at 38 East Main Street in Springfield. Business was conducted there for two years on Saturday evenings.

M&M was later located in the Edward Ryan Building, on the west side of South Limestone Street, from 1894 until March 1897, and in the Gotwald Building from March 1897 to October 18, 1919, at which time M&M purchased the structure and renamed it the M&M Building. On June 2, 1953, the institution purchased two adjoining properties, and on March 26, 1954, Edwin B. Lohnes, president and chairman of the board of directors, announced construction of a new facility south of the M&M Building. Both employees and the community celebrated its grand opening on June 27, 1955.

M&M's first branch office was opened on May 7, 1957, in Fairborn; in 1964 it moved to a newly constructed curvilinear building at 77 South Central Avenue.

In November 1971 an auto teller drive-up facility was opened adjacent to the home office. On December 17, 1973, M&M opened its North Branch office, which was located at 2000 North Limestone Street.

Additional branch offices were opened in Springfield on East Burnett Road in 1980 and on Derr Road in 1983. M&M also has two branches in Union County, in Marysville and Richwood.

The firm's original name was changed on May 23, 1908, to Merchants and Mechanics Savings and Loan Association. This name continued until April 15, 1935, when the state charter was changed by 100-percent conversion to the federal charter under which the institution now operates.

At the close of business on July 5,

The M&M Federal Savings and Loan occupied a portion of the Gotwald Building from 1897 until 1919.

1902, after ten years of operation, the assets of the association were $356,619; today it has assets of approximately $325 million. There are 128 employees working in the institution's seven offices.

Originally, M&M offered only two services to its customers, regular savings accounts and mortgage loans. Today it offers regular and statement savings accounts, interest-earning checking accounts, certificates of deposit, IRA and Keogh retirement accounts, and money management (money market) accounts. Mortgage, construction, home equity, commercial, and personal unsecured loans are also available.

Current ancillary services include direct deposit of payroll or government checks, transfer of interest from certificates of deposit to checking or savings accounts, automatic loan payments from checking accounts, and safe deposit boxes. Anticipated to be in effect in 1985 are a line of credit overdraft features for checking ac-

counts, automobile loans, and automatic-teller machines.

Eugene L. Ditmer became president of M&M Federal Savings and Loan Association in 1977, and Richard L. Kuss serves as chairman of the board.

The current site of M&M Federal Savings and Loan is at the corner of South Limestone and East Main streets.

THE KISSELL COMPANY

When Cyrus Broadwell Kissell opened a real estate business in Springfield during a time of exuberant economic expansion in 1884, his competition included twenty-four established firms. Less than ten years later The Kissell Company was considered "the most prominent enterprise of its kind in the city."

The Kissell Company, headquartered in Springfield, Ohio, is one of the nation's oldest mortgage banking firms in existence. Kissell founded his business to secure capital for people wanting to own a home at a time when real estate financing was almost nonexistent. The little money that was available for lending was not earmarked for mortgages. A down payment of 50 percent with an average term of three to five years was the only loan being offered at the time.

However, Kissell remained true to his belief "that the key to a stable community is property ownership." As a result of his efforts to make home ownership easier, his real estate business grew and prospered.

As the twentieth century ap-

C.B. Kissell—a man who paved the way for the city's progress and expansion.

The American dream has always been home ownership.

proached, Cyrus' son, Harry Seaman Kissell, joined the firm. He later became recognized as "The Elder Statesman of Real Estate" for his prominent role in providing decisive leadership for the American home-

buying public.

Harry realized a need for national professional real estate standards, so he organized the National Association of Real Estate Boards (NAREB). In 1930 he helped lead NAREB, the largest trade organization in the country, through the midst of the Great Depression. With home buying at a standstill, he helped develop the National Home Loan Bank Board, a vehicle for financing residential housing.

Harry Kissell's influence was instrumental in gaining passage of the National Housing Act of 1934, which created the Federal Housing Administration and Federal Savings and Loan Insurance Corporation (FSLIC). This legislation provided home mortgage insurance and encouraged depositors to return to financial institutions where their money would be insured.

During the early 1930s Howard Bradshaw Noonan joined The Kissell Company, bringing new and innovative ideas to the organization. Eventually named chief executive officer, Noonan worked in a unique business relationship with The Metropolitan Life Insurance Company. Kissell originated mortgages and sold them to Metropolitan as investments. This partnership paved the way for Kissell to open its first loan-originating branch in Dayton in 1937, marking The Kissell Company's beginning as a mortgage banker.

Noonan vastly expanded Kissell's market area by opening branch offices in many states for the origination of mortgages. To accommodate the abundance of new business generated by the branches, Noonan installed the first computer system used for mortgage accounting, escrow control, tax analysis, and insurance records.

With the arrival of the baby boom in the 1950s and the expansion of America's suburbs, The Kissell Company grew to become Ohio's largest mortgage-servicing firm. In the first half of that decade, Kissell serviced forty-eight million dollars in residential loans. By the end of the 1950s that figure topped $200 million.

By 1960 Kissell's residential loans more than doubled to $436 million. The company expanded from residential loans into apartments, resort properties, and industrial construction outside of the state of Ohio.

To raise much-needed capital to finance Kissell's growing business, another first was implemented in 1964: the sale of The Kissell Company stock on the American Stock Exchange. This marked the first time that a mortgage banker's stock was traded over a major stock exchange.

Still another first for the company occurred in 1967 with the sale of the first collateralized note as an investment to a pension fund. This led to the sale and servicing of the Government National Mortgage Association (GNMA) security.

Harry Kissell led a "revolution" to make home-owning dreams come true.

The 1970s brought unprecedented growth to the firm. As a part of a planned expansion, the company opened branches in the Sun Belt, on the East and West coasts, and in Alaska and Hawaii. Kissell's market area was thus transformed from a regional to a national operation.

In 1975 Robert Christie was named chief executive officer of the firm. Under his direction, The Kissell Company expanded to a fifty-branch operation in twenty-three states. Christie also assisted Kissell in the development of an array of fixed- and variable-rate residential loans, to provide a constant source of residential financing.

To meet the challenge of the 1980s, Kissell recently developed a new Correspondent Mortgage Loan Program. Through correspondents, Kissell has purchased mortgage loans originated by such financial establishments as banks, savings and loans, and credit unions. This program has helped many institutions remain in the mortgage loan business by providing affordable interest rates and discounts at no market risk. Another Kissell service is a Relocation Finance Program, which assists some of America's largest corporations by obtaining home financing for their relocating employees.

Today The Kissell Company, an affiliate of PNC Financial Corp., serves more than 250,000 customers. With a portfolio totaling seven billion dollars, the firm, which is celebrating its centennial, is still dedicated to making the American dream of owning a home a reality.

C. B. KISSELL, *Real Estate and Loans.*

Cyrus Broadwell Kissell opened a one-man real estate business in Springfield.

By the late 1960s Kissell's success had caught the eye of Pittsburgh National Corporation, the forerunner of PNC Financial Corp., and an organization with a similar financial outlook and solid capital position. The corporation was interested in becoming more involved in the financing of residential construction in the United States. The Kissell Company, closing millions of dollars in mortgages each week, needed a more solid capital base. So, in 1969, the Pittsburgh National Corporation acquired The Kissell Company.

HEAT-TREATING, INC.

Chester R. Walthall founded Heat-Treating, Inc., on July 1, 1959, when he purchased heat-treating facilities on South Thompson Avenue from the Patton Manufacturing Company. For five years the new company remained at that location. In 1964 a new 6,000-square-foot building was constructed at 1807 West Pleasant Street; but, even before construction was completed, the firm realized a need for more space and added 1,000 square feet the following year. Additional space was added in 1967, 1972, 1977, and 1979, which provided the corporation with 15,514 square feet of building space. Another major addi-

Chester R. Walthall, founder.

Chester L. Walthall, current president.

tion was completed in 1984.

Walthall, Heat-Treating's first president, was assisted by Ruth Walthall as vice-president and Frank Murphy as secretary/treasurer. Walthall's son, Chester L., purchased the firm on October 12, 1977, and is its current president. William Chiles is now plant superintendent, Carroll Johnson is vice-president, and Judy Harber is office manager.

Heat-Treating, Inc., provides production heat treating for the automotive, bicycle, truck, aerospace, material-handling, and lawn and garden industries. In addition, the firm processes a variety of such screw machine parts as bearing races, shaft-

ing, and all types of fasteners, and also has a complete tool and die hardening facility.

In 1976 Heat-Treating, Inc., acquired the assets of Precision Metal Treating, Inc., and retained its employees as well as its owner, Carroll Johnson, who was appointed sales manager of the combined operations. The merger provided a broader scope of heat-treating services and professional metallurgical advice.

Heat-Treating, Inc., thermally processed approximately 5.5 million pounds of heat-treating services through its facility in 1984. About 80 percent of all metals that are heat treated in its building are chemically changed by adding carbon, or carbon and nitrogen (carburizing, carbonitriding, or cyaniding) to the surface. The remaining 20 percent are through hardening materials that already have the chemical elements in the steel, allowing them to be hardened by heating and quenching.

Active in many community and professional organizations, Chet Walthall was presented the Silver Knight of Management Award by the National Management Association in March 1984. The firm is a member of that group as well as of the Springfield Management Association, the Springfield Area Chamber of Commerce, the United States Chamber of Commerce, the Metal Treating Institute, the Society of Manufacturing Engineers, and the Community Blood Bank. As a sustaining member of the American Society of Metals, Heat-Treating, Inc., sponsors technical courses through that society and also provides tuition reimbursement programs for its own key personnel. The firm's employees are also active participants in the United Way campaign in the Springfield area.

The offices and plant of Heat-Treating, Inc., are in facilities constructed in 1964 at 1807 West Pleasant Street.

OHIO EDISON

Arthur Zerkle, appliance section supervisor, in an automobile owned by The Springfield Light, Heat & Power Co., which operated in Springfield from 1908 to 1924. Zerkle worked for the electric company for thirty-eight years.

Word spread quickly after Thomas Edison demonstrated his electric lamp in 1879 and the 1882 opening of the first central generating station constructed to distribute electricity to users over a wide area.

Just one year later Springfield was among the first U.S. cities to have an electric power plant. Located at the Driscoll Carriage Works on Columbia Street between Fountain and Limestone, it was built by The Champion Electric Company to furnish power to several arc streetlights and a nearby retail store.

The city's use of electricity grew rapidly, and the suppliers of that power changed just as quickly. The Springfield Light and Power Company was incorporated on October 24, 1891, and one month later was deeded Champion's property.

On October 4, 1901, The Home Lighting, Power and Heating Company, a steam-heating service, was incorporated by five local residents. In its first year the firm added a generating station, the city's fourth, which obtained its cooling water from Mill Run under the city's downtown sections.

In 1905, when The Peoples Light,

Heat and Power Company, a water heating service, was formed, it acquired the property of Springfield Light and Power. The first two generating stations were abandoned, but the city's fifth was constructed at Fountain Avenue on Jefferson.

The Springfield Light, Heat & Power Co. was incorporated on September 23, 1908; it acquired Peoples on September 25 and purchased the Home Company on October 1. The new firm cut all customers over to steam and also began construction of the Rockaway Generating Station.

The Ohio Edison Company was

incorporated on May 17, 1923, and Springfield LH&P was consolidated into it the following year. With insufficient condensing water available to further expand the Rockaway plant, a station was constructed in 1927 on Mad River just south of Route 40 on the city's west edge. Two 30,000-kilowatt, oil-fired units, installed in 1972, continue to produce electric power there.

In 1930 Ohio Edison in Springfield consolidated with Northern Ohio Power and Light Company and the Akron Steam Heating Company, both of Akron; the London Light and Power Company; and the Pennsylvania-Ohio Power and Light Company of Youngstown. This merger created Ohio Edison Company, headquartered in Akron.

In 1944 Pennsylvania Power Company became a wholly owned subsidiary of Ohio Edison. The Toronto Power Plant was acquired on the Ohio River, and nine new generating units were constructed around the Edison system by 1950, when Ohio Edison merged with Ohio Public Service Company to become the largest electric firm in the state.

Walter H. Sammis was president of Ohio Edison from 1944 to 1964, a period that saw tremendous growth both for the company and the industry. Succeeding Sammis and serving until 1975, D. Bruce Mansfield oversaw the commitment to and early construction of huge generating units, including one at Shippingport, Pennsylvania.

John R. White became president in 1974, and was succeeded by Justin T. Rogers, Jr., in 1979. This ten-year period saw a massive expenditure approaching one billion dollars to meet federal and state environmental standards; the construction of nuclear power plants at Shippingport, Pennsylvania, and North Perry, Ohio; and various consumer activities aimed at assisting the needy and promoting efficient use of energy.

Philip Zerkle, son of Arthur and now a senior fieldman with Ohio Edison in Springfield, began a career with Edison in 1952. Both photos, though years apart, were shot near Warder Public Library.

TAYLOR MANUFACTURING CO., INC.

James Thomas Taylor, an inventor and designer of tools, and his son, Dale Douglas, a machinist, thought that 1939 was a good year in which to launch a business of their own. That year they opened Taylor Manufacturing Co. in a building at the rear of 530 West North Street, formerly the site of Hauck Tin Shop.

There were three employees that first year: George Thomas and James Clifton Taylor, two of James Thomas' sons, and Orma McCarty, bookkeeper and sister of James Thomas. James Clifton worked from 1940 until his death in 1972, and George Thomas became a partner in 1941. He resigned in 1947.

Taylor Manufacturing Co. performs screw machine, lathe, milling, drilling, and grinding operations. Its principal products are aircraft parts and subassemblies.

James Thomas Taylor (shown here), with his son, Dale Douglas, founded Taylor Manufacturing Co. in 1939.

The firm produces precision parts for aircraft, helicopters, missiles, and associated support equipment. Delco Products of Dayton cited Taylor Manufacturing Co. for outstanding work as a subcontractor during World War II.

One family has owned Taylor Manufacturing Co. for three generations, and members of the fourth generation are now working for the firm. More than half a dozen of Tay-lor's thirty-five employees have been with the firm for twenty-five or more years, and about half have approximately twenty years' service.

Russell S. Snook joined the company in 1947 as sales representative, and Samuel E. Day joined in 1951 as an apprentice machinist, and has been general manager since 1970. They are described by Dale Taylor as "assets to the company and to their fellow workers."

After building two additions onto the plant at 530 West North Street, Taylor Manufacturing Co. moved to its present location at 1101 West Main Street in 1958. Two new additions have been added, bringing the total area of work space to 20,000 square feet.

In 1970 Taylor Manufacturing Co. received the first of four Small Business Administration awards as National Small Business Subcontractor of the Year. These awards cited the firm's outstanding contributions and service to the nation's civilian and defense needs. The remaining awards were presented in 1973, 1974, and 1976.

Dale Douglas Taylor retired from the presidency of the company in June 1982. A son of James Thomas and Inez Felix Taylor, he had worked in the business for forty-three years. Robert Bruce and Dale Thomas are now president and vice-president, respectively, of Taylor Manufacturing Co. They are the sons of Dale D. and Mildred B. Taylor.

Taylor Manufacturing Co., Inc., has moved from the age of line-shaft, belt-driven machines into the world of high-tech computerized equipment.

The employees of Taylor Manufacturing Co., circa 1942, including George Thomas Taylor (second from left, standing), James Thomas Taylor (second from right, standing), and Dale Douglas Taylor (kneeling, far left), pose in front of the shop which was then located at the rear of 530 West North Street.

In this 1971 photo in front of the current West Main Street facility are Dale Douglas Taylor, James Clifton Taylor, and Russell S. Snook, then sales manager (far left to right). Fourth from right is Samuel E. Day, general manager. In front of him is Dale Thomas Taylor, vice-president, and on his right is Robert Bruce Taylor, president.

SOCIETY BANK, N.A.

The bank's lobby around 1953, when the bank was at 9 East Main Street.

In December 1872 a group of Springfield businessmen held a meeting and, foreseeing the future growth of the city as a manufacturing center, determined that what Springfield needed more than anything else was a savings bank.

The Springfield Savings Society was organized and subsequently opened for business on January 4, 1873, providing a place for local citizens to deposit their money or to borrow funds for home loans and farm mortgages. The mutual savings

The new main office of the Springfield Bank was completed in 1961.

societies were designed to meet the financial needs of the communities they served.

The bank's first home was in the heart of Springfield in a small room on the southwest corner of Main Street and Fountain Avenue. Known as Trapper's Corner, it was the site of a trapper's cabin during the 1840 "Tippecanoe and Tyler, Too" presidential campaign. It is interesting to note that this favorite gathering place in the heart of the city once again became the location of the Springfield Bank in 1961.

The Savings Society Commercial Bank was organized on April 20, 1956, creating two institutions under one roof. In 1965 The Springfield Bank became the new name of the Springfield Savings Society, the First State Bank of South Charleston, and the Commercial Bank. It became affiliated with the Society Corporation of Cleveland in October 1967.

Society National Bank of the Miami Valley is the result of the merger of The Springfield Bank and Xenia National Bank on December 15, 1980. In August 1984 the Society National Bank of the Miami Valley merged

The Burnett Plaza offices of Society Bank, N.A., shortly after completion in 1963.

eleven Cincinnati offices of Society National Bank of Cleveland into the six Springfield offices to form Society Bank, National Association. During 1985 Society Banks in the four major cities of southern Ohio—Columbus, Cincinnati, Dayton, and Springfield—will merge and retain the name, Society Bank, N.A.

Throughout the years Society Bank, N.A., has been a safe and secure haven for depositors' funds and the use of those funds in the local community has been a strong factor in Springfield's growth.

In 1954 the installment loan section of the bank was located in the area shown, while additional offices were situated one storefront down East Main Street.

ROBBINS & MYERS, INC.

Robbins & Myers' roots in Springfield go back more than 100 years to 1878, when Chandler Robbins, a soldier, surveyor, and astronomer, purchased the Lever Wringer Company, a gray iron foundry, for the then-princely sum of $500.

He was joined shortly thereafter by James A. Myers, first an educator and later a businessman with an enviable reputation for honesty and integrity, and the foundry was renamed the Robbins & Myers Company.

The firm's business was supplying castings to the agricultural implement market, of which Springfield was a major center. By 1884 the company had grown to thirty-five employees and approximately $25,000 in capital. In 1896 the bicycle, or "velocipede" as it was then called, craze swept the country, and Robbins & Myers began to supply castings to this multi-million-dollar national market.

But Robbins & Myers was also looking outside of the castings industry for new and more lucrative markets for its production skills. About this time the country entered the age of electricity, and the firm was convinced that electricity provided the avenue it sought to new markets.

In 1897 Robbins & Myers began manufacturing electric fans. A year

Chandler Robbins purchased the Lever Wringer Company in 1878.

later the company began simultaneously to manufacture motors for its fans, and larger motors and generators for heavy factory and production machinery. Demand mushroomed, and Robbins & Myers sold its original foundry and castings business in order to concentrate on the production of fans and motors.

The first two decades of the twentieth century were exciting years for the firm as it played a pioneering role in the development of new motor designs for labor-saving applications. Among these were small motors for washing machines, sewing machines, and vacuum cleaners; motor generator sets for the new wireless telegraph; automobile starter motors; and large, direct-current motors to power industrial machinery.

The proven success in applying motors to appliances and equipment became the cornerstone of Robbins & Myers' strategy for future growth and was first implemented in 1929

James A. Myers joined Chandler Robbins shortly after the latter purchased the Lever Wringer Company, which was renamed Robbins & Myers.

when the company formed its Hoist and Crane manufacturing operation.

Continually looking for new products that could be driven by its motors, Robbins & Myers made contact in 1932 with a French inventor named Rene J.L. Moineau, who had invented a unique pump. Operating on the progressing cavity principle, the pump was able to handle very viscous, abrasive, or corrosive materials and had excellent metering characteristics, all features not commonly found in other types of pumps available on the market.

In 1936 the firm acquired an exclusive licensing agreement for the manufacture and marketing of the pump in North America. This product, renamed the Moyno Pump after its French inventor, put Robbins & Myers in a new growth business, and the Moyno Pump Division, forerunner of today's Fluids Handling Division, was born.

Initially growth was slow, but Robbins & Myers' history of being able to solve difficult application problems began to pay dividends. One of the first major markets for the new division was the ceramic industry where Moyno Pumps were used to pump clay slips and porcelain enamels used in ceramic tiles, plumbing fixtures, pottery products, insulators, and spark plugs. Other early applications were pumping molasses, starch slurries, brewer's yeast, chocolate, corn syrups, and rubber

Rene J.L. Moineau invented the Moyno Pump.

A Moyno Pump, a product of Robbins & Myers, is used to pump makeup at a leading cosmetics company.

---

cement.

Sales to industry were curtailed severely in the early 1940s, when the demands of World War II dictated that the country's industrial might be turned to helping in the war effort. The Moyno Pump Division played its part in this effort with Moyno Pumps filling incendiary bombs with a gelatin-like mixture of soap and gasoline and hundreds more used in bilge and fire service aboard Navy and Coast Guard ships.

In 1959 the division had outgrown its cramped quarters in the Electric Motor Division facilities on Lagonda Avenue. The vacant Buckeye Bumper plant of the Electric Auto-Lite Company on West Jefferson Street was purchased and became the division's new home. Continued growth in ensuing years dictated the need for additional room, and 70,000 square feet of manufacturing space and 12,000 square feet of office space was added.

Today Robbins & Myers' Moyno Pumps are acknowledged as the

An early Moyno Progressing Cavity Pump.

standard of the industry in a wide spectrum of process industries throughout the world. In the food industry, they are used to pump cookie and bread doughs, clam chowder, peanut butter, tomato paste, potato salad, and pickle relish. In the cosmetics industry, they are used to pump hand lotions, mascara, shampoo, suntan lotion, and toothpaste.

In the paper industry, Moyno Pumps are used to pump coatings, while in the chemical industry they find application in the pumping of

latex paints, photographic emulsions, polyester blends, dyestuffs, and adhesives. In the environmental field, they are used to pump sludges, grease, and scum in municipal and industrial waste treatment plants.

Robbins & Myers Fluids Handling Division is keeping abreast of new and emerging markets, and today Moyno Pumps are used in shallow oil well service and enhanced oil recovery systems, and to pump coal/oil slurries and radioactive wastes from nuclear power plants.

Robbins & Myers, through its Fluids Handling Division, continues to be one of Springfield's major businesses with more than 500 employees and an annual payroll in excess of ten million dollars. An additional one million dollars is added to the local economy annually through purchases from area businesses.

Robbins & Myers, Inc., also continues its tradition of playing an active role in the community, a tradition begun when Charles McGilvary, the firm's second president, served as Springfield's mayor from 1913 to 1919. Today Robbins & Myers' employees and their families are active in a wide variety of community organizations and activities.

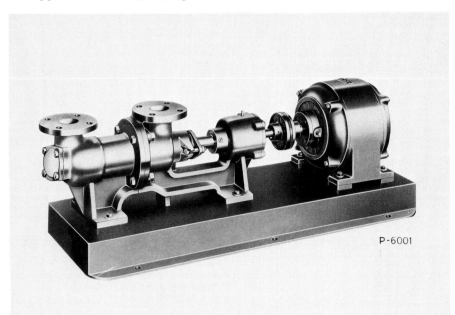

P-6001

NOLTE BRASS FOUNDRY COMPANY

In 1887 Augustus Bernard Nolte, a Cincinnati resident, became associated with MacGregor Brothers and Company, which had been established the previous year. On December 31, 1889, Nolte bought the firm from Alex MacGregor for $1,508.25 and became its sole owner. He paid $308.25 on that date and signed a note to pay $600 on December 31 of the next two succeeding years. The amount of interest was not specified in the bill of sale.

On January 1, 1890, the firm was renamed Nolte Brass Company. Seven years later a two-story brick building with basement was constructed at 21-27 West Jefferson Street. Designated Building 1, it housed the office and operations, while Building 2, erected that same year, housed the foundry operations. Buildings 3 and 4, constructed in 1912, housed the machine shop and provided space for additional melting capacity, respectively.

Nolte Brass Foundry Company was incorporated on January 5, 1923, by A.B. Nolte, Katherine Wurster Nolte, Allan A. Nolte, Wilbur H. Pence, and John M. Cole. Total sales for the month were 57,271 pounds, which produced an income of $6,745.54 and a net income of $1,236.92. In contrast, at the end of June 1980 the firm reported average

Augustus Bernard Nolte, founder.

monthly sales of 73,157 pounds, which produced an average monthly income of $289,655 and an average net income of $14,612.

In 1932 The Thompson-Owens Company of Toledo was purchased, and the entire plant was moved to Springfield. Consisting primarily of the manufacture of bronze bearings and bushings to customer specifica-

The plant and general offices of the Nolte Brass Foundry Company are located at 21-27 West Jefferson Street.

tions, the operation became a captive foundry by 1950.

Samuel Ort Nolte, son of Allan A. Nolte, became associated with the firm in 1930 as sales engineer. After World War II he became general manager and chairman of the board, a position he held until the closing of operations. Ralph H. Wetherbee, Jr., became associated with Nolte Brass Foundry Company in 1950. He later became president/treasurer, a position he also held until the closing of operations.

Some of the local customers of Nolte Brass Foundry Company included Central Brass Fixture Company, Foos Gas Engine Company, Kelly-Springfield Road Roller Company, Mast Foos Company, Robbins & Myers, Inc., Superior Gas Engine Company, and Thomas Manufacturing Company.

During 1981 and 1982 the majority of Nolte's customers experienced depressed business conditions, primarily because of high interest rates and increasing foreign imports, which led to Nolte's temporary shutdown announcement on October 22, 1982. On February 9, 1983, with business conditions still depressed, customers and employees of Nolte Brass Foundry Company were advised that the closing of all operations would be permanent as of the next day.

THE PARKER SWEEPER COMPANY

William Thomas Parker, dissatisfied with conditions in England, gathered his family and belongings and came to America in 1878. His journey ended in Springfield, at that time a center for agricultural equipment manufacturing. The town's main industry spawned the proliferation and diversification of foundries and machine shop trades and probably had a great deal to do with his coming to Springfield to resume his trade—pattern making.

On February 6, 1884, he opened a small pattern shop, The W.T. Parker Manufacturing Company, on West Washington Street. Receipts from the first day of business were twelve dollars, and he had a work force of four. Growth was slow but steady, and Parker had about twelve people working with him at the beginning of World War I.

In 1915 machine shops and foundries were busily engaged in the war effort. Edwin D. Parker joined his father, and in 1918 the firm's name was changed to The Parker Pattern Works Company.

Edwin became interested in developing a better method of clearing lawns of grass clippings and leaves than by hand raking. The result was a lawn sweeper, and a new industry in the lawn and garden field was born. However, most people at that time lived either in the city or on family-owned farms. Suburban living was still in the future.

The first recorded sale of a lawn sweeper was in 1921 in Chicago. During the late 1920s and 1930s the firm expanded by producing a total of nineteen different models. The market for its product was almost exclusively parks, cemeteries, and large estates in the larger cities. Because of this expanding business, the Springfield Lawnsweeper Company was incorporated as a separate entity and moved to its own West Clark Street address. The Parker Pattern Works Company continued operation, but

The Parker Sweeper Company offices and plant at 91 Bechtle Avenue.

at a new location in the Greenawalt Industries Building at 100 West Main Street.

During World War II production of lawn and floor sweepers was not permitted. In 1942 the two concerns combined into The Parker Pattern and Foundry Company and moved to the present Bechtle Avenue address. The firm's war efforts went in two directions. A large mechanized magnesium foundry was installed to provide magnesium castings for aircraft. And, in conjunction with Wright-Patterson Air Force Base in Dayton, Parker developed and manufactured a calibration stand for the famous Norden bombsight.

In 1944 Richard W. Parker, grandson of the founder, became general manager. Postwar trends toward suburban living and larger lawns made the country ready for the lawn sweeper. As a result, Parker began organizing and coordinating all engineering, production, sales, and marketing efforts toward developing a lawn sweeper for home use.

In 1948 the firm's name was changed to The Parker Sweeper Company, and additional models, including powered lawn sweepers, lawn blowers, vacuums, air blowers, Thatch-O-Matic power rakes, and the Trail-Vac were introduced. During the early 1950s distribution rapidly expanded from coast to coast, and by the mid-1950s Parker began to develop a solid export market in Europe, South America, Africa, and the Far East. The current Parker line of turf and hard-surface maintenance equipment is sold to consumers and to commercial and industrial users.

CREDIT LIFE INSURANCE COMPANY

Credit Life Insurance Company, organized in September 1925 by a group of forward-thinking businessmen who were then associated with the Morris Plan Bank (now Security National Bank), began operations on February 1, 1926, when it issued the first group credit life insurance policy to be issued in the United States. The organizers felt that they could offer an additional service to customers by automatically liquidating an individual's indebtedness should death occur prior to the termination of the customer's financial obligation to the bank. Five employees were guided by founder and president Ralph W. Hollenbeck, who headed the company until 1938.

Once Credit Life was formed, it seemed appropriate to expand its operation by soliciting other institutions in Ohio and adjacent states to use its facilities. During the late 1920s Credit Life experienced gradual growth through the acquisition of other lending institutions.

World War II saw the decreasing manufacture of consumer goods, and the company's growth stagnated. However, in the mid-1940s, when the economy was returning to a peaceful environment and consumer products were reappearing, the institution's growth also began to rise.

Credit Life's growth continued to accelerate through the 1950s and until the mid-1960s through the combined efforts of the firm's personnel and independent insurance agents who, for the first time, became a factor in its markets. Before the 1960s most all production had been developed by company personnel; this changed when independent agents began marketing Credit Life's products.

Today Credit Life's products are essentially group or individual life and disability coverage, offered in more than a dozen varieties. These insurance coverages are issued in connection with lending transactions originating from consumer loan companies, commercial banks, savings banks, mortgage bankers, savings and loan associations, and such vendors or retailers as automobile dealers and furniture stores.

In late 1975, with its business growing rapidly, Credit Life constructed and moved into a four-story building at 100 South Limestone Street. In 1973 the firm purchased the Toledo National Insurance Company, a property and casualty concern, which it renamed the Credit General Insurance Company. In 1980 Credit Life moved into a new steel-and-glass, ten-story facility at the corner of East Main and South Limestone streets.

Credit Life, which had only $860,470 of insurance in force at the end of 1926, has $12.6 billion in force

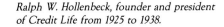

Ralph W. Hollenbeck, founder and president of Credit Life from 1925 to 1938.

The current home of Credit Life Insurance Company, at the corner of Main and Limestone streets, was opened in 1981.

today. It frequently leads the field among its competitors in having the most insurance in force in a given year. There are currently 591 employees in the firm's home office in Springfield.

Credit Life Insurance Company's presidents, following its founder, have been John F. Hollenbeck, from 1938 to 1949; Dwight W. Hollenbeck, currently chairman of the board, from 1950 to 1965; William Ultes, Jr., from 1966 to 1973; and Forrest J. Curtin, since 1973.

McGREGOR METALWORKING COMPANIES

"If business isn't fun, we don't do it," says John C. McGregor, Sr. This entrepreneurial spirit came from McGregor's grandfather, Frank McGregor, who, with his brother David, was a late nineteenth-century Springfield entrepreneur florist with a retail mail-order catalog. In those days Springfield was called the "Rose City."

John and his four sons, John C. Jr. "Jack," Daniel P., James B., and Thomas W., own and operate four local plants that are contract manufacturers of metal parts. This third- and fourth-generation entrepreneurial spirit began in 1965 when John McGregor purchased a small tool and die shop, Morgal Machine Tool Co., from Frank Morgal, a neighbor and good friend. At the time of the purchase, John Sr. was employed by Mast-Foos Mfg. Co. (The year 1985 will mark his fiftieth anniversary in the metalworking industry.) He called upon Jack, his oldest son, to manage his newly acquired company. Three years later Dan joined his brother. When John Sr. retired from Mast-Foos in 1970, he also became active in the management of Morgal. Jim and Tom joined Morgal in 1973 and 1978, respectively.

Morgal is a contract metal stamper, specializing in the manufacture of stamped steel sprockets and assemblies. Its markets include bicycle, lawn and garden, conveyor, and overhead door companies. Today Morgal is managed by John Sr., Dan, and Jim and is located at 2100 South Yellow Springs Street.

In 1972 Jack struck out on his own and formed Pentaflex, Inc., located at 701 East Columbia Street. Pentaflex is a contract metal stamping company that also has a complete tool- and die-making facility. The bulk of its work is for the truck axle industry. Pentaflex also supplies the electrical equipment and building-products industries. Pentaflex has stamping press capacity up to 1,000 tons.

Back row, from left: John C. "Jack" McGregor, Jr.; John C. McGregor, Sr.; and Dan McGregor. Front row, from left: Tom McGregor and Jim McGregor.

Morgal bought stamping equipment and a building located at 1305 Innisfallen Avenue from International Harvester Company in 1980 and created Ohio Stamping and Machine, Inc. (OSMI), as a wholly owned subsidiary. OSMI manufactures medium to large metal stampings and single-spindle screw machine products and serves the automotive, agricultural, and bicycle industries.

In 1982 Tom purchased Carmichael Machine Corporation, located at 5573 West National Road. Carmichael is a contract manufacturer of precision-machine parts for the military, appliance, and automotive industries. Carmichael has two primary departments, one utilizing computerized numerically controlled machining centers, and the other using multiple-spindle screw machines and related equipment for general machine work.

When John bought Morgal Machine in 1965, there were five employees and that year's total sales amounted to $55,000. In 1984 the four separate companies had 152 employees, and total sales of fourteen million dollars. Needless to say, John and his four sons have maintained the entrepreneurial spirit of Frank McGregor.

ST. JOHN'S CENTER

St. John's Center, a nonprofit, non-denominational, skilled-care nursing and convalescent facility, opened its doors at 100 West McCreight Avenue on October 1, 1976, as St. John's Nursing and Convalescing Home.

This 150-bed facility, the dream of its founder, the Reverend Kay Medick Glaesner, Jr., pastor of the city's St. John's Evangelical Lutheran Church, provides skilled health care to meet the physical, mental, spiritual, social, and rehabilitative needs of its residents. Pastor Glaesner, recognizing the need for a holistic, extended-care facility in Clark County, called members of his church together in 1970 and presented the concept to them.

During the next five years he enlisted the assistance of virtually hundreds of people. The Sisters of Mercy, whose Mercy Medical Center is adjacent to St. John's, donated the 5.3 acres of land on which the center stands. The Friends of St. John's Center, whose purpose is to raise funds to assist the center in providing health-care services, was organized in January 1976. The organization continues to assist the center and Oakwood Village.

The first administrator of the cen-

The Reverend Kay Medick Glaesner, Jr., Sc.D., who, while serving for more than thirty-five years as pastor of Springfield's St. John's Evangelical Lutheran Church, founded St. John's Center and Oakwood Village of St. John's.

ter was Andrew L. Turner. Under the chairmanship of Walter Gartman, the original board of trustees included William G. Baldenhofer, Donald J. Bishop, Keith M. Bruster, John L.

St. John's Center, 100 West McCreight Avenue.

Cashin, Paul F. Hellmuth, Neal E. Kresheck, David D. Mattes, Jack F. Miller, Joseph D. Myers, Howard B. Noonan, Robert H. Pequignot, William H. Ruef, Robert W. Wray, and Merrill B. Wells. The facility's second administrator was Thomas L. Howard. He was followed by Gary L. Wade, the present administrator. Marianne S. Wildermuth, who worked during the years of planning for the center's opening, is assistant administrator.

St. John's Center was the first extended-care facility in Ohio to have a 24-hour, in-house pharmacy and a full-time respiratory therapy staff.

Residents of the center, who have ranged in age from a few months to more than 100 years, are served by health-care professionals and by volunteers. In 1984 volunteers donated more than 19,000 hours of service to the residents.

An adult day-care program, funded through the Clark County Mental Health Board, offers a comprehensive program of social activities, as well as all nursing and therapy services Monday through Friday. Participants return to their homes in the community in the evenings.

A St. John's Center Auxiliary, composed of men and women of the community who band together in fund-raising projects that benefit the center's residents with new equipment and furniture, has highlighted each fall season with its Wine and Cheese Festival.

St. John's Center has an open admissions policy. Residents are admitted without regard to race, color, sex, national origin, or religious affiliation.

Through the efforts of the current board of trustees, Oakwood Village of St. John's, located at 1500 Villa Road, is under construction. Oakwood Village, a continuing-care retirement community, will have about 150 apartments and cottages, and a health-care center.

THE ELLIOTT COMPANY

In 1892 Gustav Wiedeke, Sr., began a small manufacturing business in Dayton. At the turn of the century a young mechanical engineer, William Swan Elliott, patented a water motor and a freely swinging arm head, which could be used effectively to clean scale and deposits from boiler tubes. He pooled his capital and organized the Liberty Manufacturing Company in Pittsburgh to produce the boiler tube cleaners. These two firms would later intertwine in two different ways with what is now The Elliott Company.

Meanwhile, in 1898 Henry F. Weinland, chief engineer of Springfield's Warder, Bushnell, and Glessner Company (later International Harvester), was also interested in how to remove scale and deposits from boiler tubes. He, too, devised a plan for a boiler tube cleaner. With Elmer Grove, a machinist, he made several of these devices and began to sell them to area manufacturers. Soon a local businessman, H.S. Bradley, joined the two men, and another tube-cleaner enterprise was under way.

The first company headquarters was the basement of Bradley's home, where the cleaners were prepared for shipment. After Grove dropped out of the business, James W. Gunn, Bradley's father-in-law, joined Weinland and Bradley in the partnership.

In 1900 they opened a small shop in the Patrick Furnace Building on West Washington Street, and two

The offices and plant of The Elliott Company, a subsidiary of United Technologies Corporation, are located at 1809 Sheridan Avenue.

years later incorporated as The Lagonda Manufacturing Company. The products, known as Weinland's Cleaners, sold briskly. Early in 1903, because of expanding business, a two-story plant was erected on East Washington Street. When Lagonda outgrew that factory, it purchased a site on Sheridan Avenue and built a new plant in 1905. That structure has been enlarged and remodeled many times and still serves as a manufacturing facility for Elliott.

In 1916 Elliott acquired Lagonda and all its stock, uniting it with his company, although Lagonda continued to operate from Springfield under its own name.

Upon founder Bradley's death in 1929, Maurice Sellers became president and successfully led the company, with minimal layoffs, during the Great Depression.

During World War II Lagonda

Employees of The Lagonda Manufacturing Company, now The Elliott Company, are shown outside the plant on July 1, 1930.

geared up to make tube-cleaning and -expanding equipment for U.S. railroads and refineries and tube tools for the Navy and the Merchant Marines. V.H. Baker led Lagonda through the 1940s and early 1950s and was followed as general manager by Lewis A. Kunzler, who served until retiring in 1976. William C. Sears was vice-president and general manager from 1976 until his retirement in 1984; he was succeeded by Joseph W. Smith.

Meanwhile, a number of changes had occurred. In 1957 Elliott's plants all became a division of Carrier Corporation, which in turn became part of United Technologies Corporation in the late 1970s. In 1969 Elliott acquired the Gustav Wiedeke Company and its line of expanding and burnishing tools.

The Elliott Company's products include tube cleaners and tube expanders, which are manufactured on Sheridan Avenue. Assembly, storage, marketing, and distribution of high-pressure pumping and water-blasting equipment and bow and stern thrusters for the maritime industry takes place at Elliott's East National Road plant.

ST. RAPHAEL CHURCH

The first Catholic church in Clark County was established in Springfield in 1849 and named to honor the Archangel Raphael. Today, 136 years later, it continues to serve many of the residents of Springfield, some of whom trace their ancestry back to the small band of Catholic families who began immigrating to Springfield about 1835.

The first Catholic settlers in Springfield were principally of German and Irish descent. These first Catholics were ministered to by the infrequent visits of itinerant priests.

The Diocese of Cincinnati, established in 1821, encompassed the huge wilderness territory that now includes Ohio, Indiana, Illinois, Michigan, and Wisconsin. The few priests who served the fledgling diocese traveled that immense territory with chalice and vestments in their saddlebags, eager to celebrate Mass and administer sacraments wherever they found Catholic settlers. The first recorded Mass in Springfield was celebrated in the home of William Griblenhoff by the Reverend Henry Damien Juncker, the pastor of Emmanuel Church in Dayton, some forty miles from Springfield.

From 1845 on, Springfield saw an increasing number of Catholic immigrants, mainly of Irish descent. They came as unskilled laborers and built the roads, canals, and railroads that began to crisscross the newly formed state.

There was a large enough number of Catholics in Springfield in 1849 to demand the attention of a resident pastor. Recognizing that need, the Bishop of Cincinnati, the Most Reverend John B. Purcell, established St. Raphael Parish and appointed the Reverend James Kearney as its first pastor in August 1849. The previous year ground had been purchased and work had begun on the construction of a church building on High Street east of Spring Street.

Father Kearney was succeeded in 1850 by the Reverend Maurice Howard, whose pastorate extended over the next thirteen years. During that time the first Catholic school in Springfield was opened in the basement of St. Raphael Church.

By 1850 Springfield boasted a population of 7,314 and was a bustling town at the end of the National Road. The Catholic population kept pace with the growing population of the city, and by 1860 a second parish was established to respond to the needs and desires of the German-speaking Catholics who wanted to hear the gospel in their own language.

Six years later a new parish was established in South Charleston (St. Charles Borromeo), but was served by the pastor of St. Raphael Parish.

The interior of St. Raphael Church, 1984.

That same year the original St. Raphael Church was remodeled and enlarged to accommodate the growing congregation. In 1864 a small frame school building had been erected, but by 1876 it was overcrowded and a new three-story brick facility was under construction.

Within four years the Catholic population was too large to be accommodated by the church and school facilities at St. Raphael's. A large number of Catholics lived in the southeastern part of the city around the East Street shops. Consequently, plans were laid in 1881 for the establishment of a third Catholic parish in Springfield, to be called St. Joseph's.

Still, the congregation at St. Raphael's continued to grow, and in 1889, under the leadership of Reverend William H. Sidley, it was determined that a new church would be built. Additional property was purchased to the west of the church to accommodate the expansion.

Charles Creager, an eminent Springfield architect, was hired to design the new facility. Demolition of the old church began on May 30, 1892, and the new foundations were laid in July. By October 1893 the new church was under roof, and the bell from the old church was hung in the smaller of the two towers. Work on the basement was completed in time for the first Mass to be sung in the new church on Christmas morning, 1893.

The rapid pace of progress was abruptly halted, however, when the allowable limit of indebtedness of $25,000 was reached in 1894. Some additional work was done the following year, but hard economic times again halted work in 1896. Work resumed in 1897 and was finally completed the following year. Amid much solemnity, the new church was dedicated on July 17, 1898, by Arch-

The original church and rectory were at the corner of High and Spring streets.

bishop William Henry Elder.

For thirty-eight years, from 1904 until 1942, the life of St. Raphael Parish was directed by the Reverend Daniel A. Buckley. He served the parish briefly as an assistant pastor in 1885-1886 and then returned as pastor in 1904. During his pastorate, the parish facilities were repeatedly expanded and improved. In 1911 construction was begun on a new school building, and ten years later the number of classrooms was doubled by an addition to the original structure.

Until 1931 St. Raphael, St. Bernard, and St. Joseph parishes all conducted a high school in addition to their elementary schools. In 1929 the three high schools began to consolidate, a process that was completed two years later with the establishment of Catholic Central High School in the St. Raphael facilities. It remained there until a new high school was constructed in 1958 at 1200 East High Street.

In 1920 Father Buckley was named to the rank of Domestic Prelate, and in 1924 he became Vicar General of the Archdiocese of Cincinnati. As such, Monsignor Buckley was the highest ranking official of the Archdiocese next to the Archbishop.

Two other Catholic parishes were established in Springfield: St. Mary's in 1921, and St. Teresa's in 1931. St. Martin Chapel was also established as a mission of St. Raphael Parish in 1943 to minister to the black Catholic population of Springfield. This small chapel was located at the corner of South Center and West Pleasant streets. In the mid 1950s it was closed, and its parishioners were assimilated into the already established parishes.

Clark County is presently served by seven parishes, five of which are in the city of Springfield. All originate from the original St. Raphael Parish.

Because of its distinctive architec-

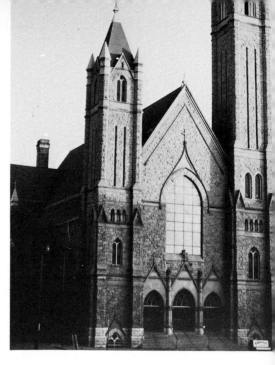

St. Raphael Church, 1984.

tural style, St. Raphael Church was nominated by the Ohio Historical Society for inclusion on the National Register of Historic Places. This distinction was accorded St. Raphael Church on June 22, 1976.

The interior of the church is a modified Gothic architectural style with a ceiling of graceful arches meeting not in columns, but in beautiful drops. The original wooden altars and communion rail were replaced in the second decade of the twentieth century by altars, railing, statues, and pulpit of matching Carrara marble and white onyx imported from Italy. The massive pulpit, made of solid marble, was carved in Florence, Italy, and took three years to complete.

The church also contains an exceptional collection of stained glass windows designed and executed by F.X. Zettler in Munich, Germany. These windows were made in 1919, and represent a high point in the art of painted glass craftsmanship. Ten eighteen- by five-foot Zettler windows grace the nave of the church.

The exterior is constructed of Berea sandstone. Its facade features two unequal towers, the taller rising to a height of 184 feet, while the smaller is 135 feet high. St. Raphael Church occupies one of the highest points in the city and is visible from nearly all directions.

SPRINGFIELD TIRE & BATTERY, INC.

April 13, 1924, a Friday, was not the traditionally unlucky day for Howard H. Detrick. That was the day he opened the Springfield Battery Company, at 315 West Main Street in a building now occupied by Monte Zinn Chevrolet. That was the beginning of a business that has been owned and operated by his family for more than sixty years.

Detrick's ancestors had come to the United States four generations earlier and had stressed to each new generation the importance of the old German work ethic. As a result, Detrick and his wife, Emelie "Pape," were no strangers to the hard work that would be required to operate the new business.

Springfield Battery was founded during a period when Henry Ford had begun mass producing the Model A and the Model T so that more Americans could afford the luxury of an automobile. During the late 1920s and the early 1930s Springfield Battery's main business was car storage, pumping gasoline, car washing, and recharging batteries.

By 1933 the firm had expanded and moved from its original location to 236 West Main Street. Business gradually increased further during these years with the addition of auto parts sales and car road service.

Springfield was not exempt from the many life-style adjustments that plagued the entire country during World War II. Gas coupons were in great demand, and convoys would

Howard H. Detrick, founder of the Springfield Battery Company (now Springfield Tire & Battery), by the company truck in front of Memorial Hall.

line up for two blocks on Main Street to buy gas at Springfield Tire & Battery. Used auto parts were in great demand as car production was stopped totally from 1941 to 1945 while plants produced tanks and Army trucks. Help was also difficult to find during the war years as most available men were drafted into the armed services.

Following World War II auto parts became a specialized field as cars changed models every year and inventories increased greatly in order to cover all vehicles coming off the assembly lines. By the 1950s the city of Springfield and Springfield Tire & Battery were both growing.

The firm's original building was located on West Main Street where Monte Zinn Chevrolet Company is now situated. The business was opened on April 13, 1924—a Friday.

That growth ceased abruptly in December 1957 when the Crowell-Collier Publishing Company closed its doors, and 2,500 Springfielders were, with no warning, out of work. It took nine years for Springfield Tire & Battery to recover its sales to the 1956 level.

The company offered 24-hour car service until 1964, when changing traffic patterns and buying habits made it wise to change its emphasis. By 1968 Springfield Tire & Battery changed from the business of repairing cars to an auto parts store specializing in servicing the walk-in customer and in delivery service to auto dealers.

On May 11, 1968, something happened that had never happened before and has not happened since. Springfield Tire & Battery was closed for the day because of the death of founder Howard H. Detrick. Since then, the firm has been incorporated by Detrick's three children, Orva and Howard John, who work six days a week in the business, and their sister, Emily Detrick Ulery.

Springfield Tire & Battery opened a store on South Limestone Street in 1972 and one in Park Layne in 1976.

SPRINGFIELD NEWSPAPERS, INC.

In the fabric of life that stretches across this nation, few things are as inextricably bound together as a newspaper and the community it serves. A study of the nation and its press will find most newspapers among the oldest continuing enterprises in their town. And so it is with the *News-Sun* and Springfield.

Newspaper history in Springfield dates back 168 years to 1817 when *The Farmer* was founded by George Smith. It endured several name changes, becoming *The Republic* in 1839, when the arrival of the National Road changed life in the community. As newspapers came and went or were absorbed by competitors, it finally became *The Press-Republic.*

Meanwhile, in 1894, through the efforts of workers in the composing and editorial rooms of other newspapers, a competitor, *The Daily Morning Sun,* was published.

Five years into the twentieth century former Ohio Governor James A. Cox, owner of the *Dayton News,* bought *The Press-Republic* and another Springfield paper, *The Daily Democrat,* combined them, and called his publication *The Spring-*

An artist's sketch of the Springfield Newspapers building at the northeast corner of North Limestone and East North Street.

field Daily News. President Woodrow Wilson pushed a button in the White House in 1915 that started the paper's mammoth presses rolling in a new plant in Springfield.

Although Cox did well, increasing expenses made it apparent that Springfield could not support two separate newspaper ownerships. At the urging of many, including local merchants, Cox bought *The Daily Morning Sun* in 1928. The following year Cox dedicated a building at the corner of Limestone and North streets to house the editorial offices of the two papers.

But, as technology ushers in a new era, it also sets the timer that will define the limits of its own reign. In this instance it was the era of hot type, which had moved from being handled by humans to automation but had remained essentially the same—rubbing ink onto a plate and then putting it to paper.

In 1975 the era of cold type and the computer came to Springfield newspapers. Gone was the clacking

of typewriters and Linotypes that set the hot metal type, and reporters began writing their stories on video display terminals. Printing now relies on a chemical process, the ink sticking only to the places on the mat where it is supposed to stick.

Economic times changed as well, and further consolidation of newspaper operations again came to Springfield in 1982 when *The Springfield Daily News* and *The Springfield Sun,* which since 1929 had published together only on Sundays, became *The Springfield News-Sun.*

Since then a new generation of computers has come to the *News-Sun.* Laser machines send photographs, and teletypes seldom sound, for all the stories are being fed silently into the new grand machine of still another new technological area.

But the Cox name is still with the publications, now having survived almost eighty years in Springfield's newspaper history, surpassing the name "Republic" in its tenure. A five-unit offset press prints a daily newspaper that is circulated to more than 40,000 people in Clark, Champaign, Logan, Madison, and Greene counties.

CONTINENTAL CABLEVISION, INC.

Amos B. Hostetter, co-founder and president.

H.I. Grousbeck, co-founder and chairman of the board.

Amos B. Hostetter and H.I. Grousbeck started Continental Cablevision in Tiffin, Ohio, in 1963. With antennas mounted on a 520-foot tower, they were able to provide a wider variety of channels and better reception. Twelve years later Hostetter is president and Grousbeck is chairman of the board of Continental Cablevision, Inc., which currently serves about 300 communities in thirteen states and employs more than 2,000 people. The corporate headquarters is located in Boston, Massachusetts, with Ohio headquarters in Findlay.

Continental came to Springfield in 1973. Initially the firm erected a building in downtown Springfield—one of the first in the urban-renewal project—to house operations that would be convenient for its customers and to show the community that it was committed to the area. Construction of the cable system began that same year, and service was provided to Continental's first customers in 1975.

The Springfield system is one of twenty-seven Continental Cablevision systems in Ohio, and from the Southern District office at 1240 East Main Street in Springfield, district manager Richard Wiegand-Moss oversees operations in Springfield, Xenia, Fairborn, Athens, Crestline, Galion, and Upper Sandusky.

At the end of 1975, the first operating year, there were 11,471 Continental customers in Springfield. Skip Lycan, Springfield system manager, and his staff of thirty full- and part-time employees currently work with some 22,000 basic cable subscribers. In addition, there are almost 10,000 HBO and more than 4,000 Cinemax subscribers in the Springfield system.

Springfield has a dual cable system, which was innovative in 1975. Two cables were laid side by side, allowing Springfielders to have the same channel capacity that is common in much larger cities. The system is flexible, permitting Continental to upgrade it continually. In 1975 the firm offered its customers twenty-four channels; early in 1985 this was expanded to forty-two channels.

Cable television, used purely for reception in the mountains of Pennsylvania during the late 1940s, now provides entertainment, information, education, and consumer services. Of particular benefit to the community are Continental's emergency alerts, telecasts of the Springfield City Commission meetings, and public, governmental, and educational access channels of local origination. All these services are offered today, by satellite and microwave, as well as antennae.

Continental Cablevision, the eighth-largest cable company in the nation, was selected by the Springfield City Commission over others bidding for the franchise because of the firm's strong record of service. Continental's corporate history shows that all franchises it has ever had have been renewed, none have been revoked, and none have been sold to another company. Continental's record in Springfield resulted in the city commission deregulating its rates in 1979.

THE P.D. COSMOS COMPANY

One of twenty retail stores of The P.D. Cosmos Company displayed the ice cream sign that caused people to call the business "Velvet." This store was on Wayne Avenue in Dayton in 1936.

Peter D. Cosmos opened a delicatessen in a small storeroom at the southwest corner of West Main and Plum streets in 1918. Each year he bought the next storeroom to the west to expand his business, and in 1926 he incorporated as The P.D. Cosmos Company. He then began the manufacture of ice cream, which he called "Velvet." This became the name by which most people called the company.

Ice cream cones were sold at five cents each. A spade spoon was used to cut each portion from the bulk ice cream. Public approval was so overwhelming that on warm summer evenings the crowd was large enough to require the police to direct traffic at the Main and Plum intersection.

Cosmos originated the concept of selling direct to the consumer through his own retail outlets. By this method he could sell at a cheaper price and the customer could more easily afford to buy ice cream. Prior to World War II he operated twenty stores in Springfield, Dayton, Xenia, Urbana, Troy, and Piqua.

Because of the shortage of man-

power during the war, the number of stores was reduced to fourteen. Hand dipping of ice cream was discontinued. All ice cream was put in packages direct from the freezer. Self service by the customer became the norm.

After the war Cosmos initiated a system in which the handling of the milk—from the farmer's cow to the dairy to the gallon jug—was automated and not touched by human hands. Milk flowed from the cow to a refrigerated holding tank at the farm to a refrigerated tank truck to a

refrigerated holding tank in the dairy to the glass gallon jug and then to the retail store.

In 1959 a gallon of Cosmos Grade A homogenized milk sold for fifty-eight cents, and a gallon of Velvet ice cream cost one dollar.

Due to ill health, Cosmos sold the business to Consolidated Foods Corporation of Chicago in August 1959. Consolidated had also purchased the Lawson Milk Company of Cuyahoga

Falls, Ohio, and the two firms were integrated under the Lawson name.

Peter Cosmos believed that the public and his employees would be well taken care of by the new owner of his company, stressing, "I have taken care of the people of Springfield and they have taken care of me."

When the Lawson Company did not renew the lease on the West Main and Plum streets property, Cosmos gave it to the Springfield Greek Orthodox Church. In 1976 the church sold it to the Monte Zinn Chevrolet Company.

The P.D. Cosmos Company, on West Main and Plum streets, when about half of the building had been remodeled.

Peter D. Cosmos, founder.

GRAPHIC PAPER PRODUCTS CORPORATION

In 1891 Charles E. Miller set up his press at 10 Zimmerman Block with the modest intent of providing good printing for Springfield customers. In 1917 he moved his presses to the Barrett Building at 108 West Columbia Street and kept on growing. Today Miller Printing Company serves clients throughout Ohio as the energizing nucleus of the printing, packaging, and publishing corporation with worldwide influence.

Miller sold his business to John E. Sparrow in 1940. Four years later Richard W. Heckler joined the firm and became its owner in 1950, upon the untimely death of Sparrow, his father-in-law. Heckler expanded the operations, acquiring Bauer Press from the estate of Wilfred Bullock in 1952.

Packaging became a part of the business in 1958 with the acquisition of the 73-year-old Rhoades Paper Box Company when the Edward Finsley-Donald Campbell partnership was dissolved. Under the direction of R.E. Aleshire, it outgrew its quarters at 66 St. John's Place and was relocated in 1964 to 109 West North Street, adjacent to the Miller Works on Columbia Street.

Other companies were added to the enterprise in 1968: Ampersand Press (formerly Antioch Press), founded in Yellow Springs in 1923 by Arthur Morgan, then president of Antioch College; and Buckeye Press, with its Wood Construction Publishing Company, founded in Xenia in 1921 by Findley M. Torrence, Sr. Ampersand's functions were absorbed into those of Buckeye Press and Miller Printing in 1970.

Fire ravaged Buckeye Press in 1971. Its equipment was moved to Springfield, and its customers were served from a sales office on West Second Street in Xenia until 1974. Much of the city, including that office, was demolished by a tornado in April of that year. All Buckeye personnel and functions were immediately moved to

Pictured during the early 1900s are (left to right) Jim McClane; Charles E. Miller, founder; and Jerry Miller.

Springfield.

That same year the name Graphic Paper Products Corporation was adopted. Barbara Allen, a key member of the Xenia operations, is now manager of corporate accounting and computer support activities.

Also in 1974 the Visual Education Association (Vis-Ed), founded in Dayton in 1950, became a part of the enterprise. The publishing of card format study aids began a new phase of vitality under the management of David Davis in 1976. With the participation of Jeanne A. Lampe, Heckler's daughter, it has expanded to worldwide recognition, with distributors in Taiwan, Singapore, and London, as well as in Los Angeles and Baltimore.

The printing and publishing activities were moved into a larger facility at 581 West Leffel Lane in 1976, and the Rhoades division was expanded into the Columbia Street plant.

Armstrong Instant Print was acquired from Howard Armstrong in 1977. Serving its own clientele and also cooperating with the major printing works, it is located at 222 East Main Street.

The Springfield Commercial Printing Company, formerly owned by Gordon Rosenberry, was brought

into the conglomerate in 1981, and in June of that year it merged with the Leffel Lane printing functions.

Barrett Brothers, Legal Publishers, which has provided legal forms for use in Ohio courts since 1860, became a part of the corporation in 1984. Its work continues in the Leffel Lane location under the direction of twin brothers Richard and Robert Barrett.

The Springfield Packaging Company, located at 2864 Columbus Avenue, became the newest member of the group in October 1984. Specializing in the manufacturing of corrugated boxes and in custom packaging services, it is managed by former owner Jon Stephenson, who is assisted by Heckler's son-in-law, Kari Lampe.

Beginning as Charles E. Miller Printers in 1891, loyal clients and several generations of dedicated craftsmen and managers have expanded the enterprise into the Graphic Paper Products Corporation, which in 1985 employed 130 people working in more than 125,000 square feet of plant and office space.

JANITOR EQUIPMENT COMPANY (JANECO)

In July 1944 Homer McFadden founded the Janitor Equipment Company at 2141 West Main Street in Springfield. During the day McFadden waited on customers; at night he produced sweeping compound in the back room of the store. McFadden, who came to Springfield to study business at Wittenberg, had purchased sanitary products for the government prior to World War II. Early records indicate a net of $180 per month in 1944.

When the company needed more space, McFadden moved his business to its present location at 1000 Dayton Avenue in 1954, where Janitor Equipment Company now has more than 6,400 square feet of space.

Donald E. Martin was employed by McFadden as a truck driver in

Homer McFadden, left, founder of Janitor Equipment Company, poses with the current owner, Donald E. Martin, outside the firm's headquarters at 1000 Dayton Avenue, Springfield.

1959, and in 1971 became sole owner of Janitor Equipment Company—now known as Janeco. In 1984 Janeco had ten employees and gross sales of more than $1,250,000.

Janeco serves Clark County and eight other counties with sanitary supplies and equipment sales for industry, institutions, hospitals, nursing

The machine shop as it looked when Janitor Equipment Company purchased the facility in 1954. The building, at 1000 Dayton Avenue, still serves as its headquarters.

homes, and schools. Janeco's products include hand-type scrub brushes, as well as sophisticated machinery that does the work of a mop and a brush all in one operation.

There are more than 1,000 different types of cleansing products available to institutional customers through Janeco, including products to clean ovens, floors, carpets, and upholstery, as well as to clear drains.

In 1959, when Martin came to the firm as an employee, waxes were made from the carnauba plant. Now they are made from synthetic materials.

Janeco includes among its customers such area industries as Robbins & Myers, Inc.; International Harvester; the SPECO Division, Kelsey-Hayes Company; and many others.

TED BOLLE MILLWORK, INC.

Theodore B.H. Bolle, Jr., began producing millwork in Yellow Springs, Ohio, in 1953, and today he and his wife Hilda R., are the sole owners of Ted Bolle Millwork, Inc. This Springfield company ships custom-made millwork across the continental United States and also to such foreign countries as Australia, England, and Belgium.

Ted Bolle Millwork's present building at 2834 Hustead Road was opened in 1961 and provided an office area and one mill section. Today, with four additions to the original mill area, there are 38,000 square feet of space available to the firm.

The thirty-five company em-

ployees are primarily involved in commercial and institutional millwork, although they sometimes work with fine residential millwork, as well. All millwork is fabricated according to architects' drawings and

Keeping up with the latest in woodworking machinery has helped Ted Bolle Millwork to stay in the forefront of the industry in Springfield and the surrounding area.

Ted Bolle Millwork, Inc., opened an office and one mill section at 2834 Hustead Road in 1961. With four subsequent additions, the facility now encompasses 38,000 square feet.

meet customer specifications.

Ted Bolle Millwork handles architectural woodwork and special wood products for any exposed wood in any building, interior or exterior.

Being in the "old line" of custom production, the company makes anything from fancy sash, doors, and all types of cabinetwork, to solid wood stairs. Straight and circular stairs, for example, are completely manufactured at the Hustead Road plant and are then shipped to the customer's site for installation. The firm also does some manufacturing of dimension stock (parts run to profile) for companies that supply kitchen cabinets and chalkboards.

Although many of the other old-line mills are out of business, including those that existed in nearby cities, Ted Bolle Millwork, Inc., has lasted and grown through the years. Today, in addition to vast production of hardwood trim and molding, the company also manufactures high-pressure laminate (formica) cabinetry for various institutions.

The firm provides not only commercial and institutional millwork, but fine residential woodwork as well.

Patrons

The following individuals, companies, and organizations have made a valuable commitment to the quality of this publication. Windsor Publications and the Clark County Historical Society and Wittenberg University gratefully acknowledge their participation in *Springfield and Clark County: An Illustrated History.*

Berryhill Nursery Co.
Ted Bolle Millwork, Inc.*
Paul Stafford Buchanan, M.D.
Clark Technical College*
Continental Cablevision, Inc.*
The P.D. Cosmos Company*
Credit Life Insurance Company*
CSS Associates, Inc.
CSS Computer Center
The Elliott Company*
Friends of the Library Genealogical
 Research Group
Graphic Paper Products Corporation*
Heat-Treating, Inc.*
Janitor Equipment Company (Janeco)*
The Kissell Company*
Harry and Marge Laybourne
Arthur and Martha Lutz
Arthur Lytle, Jr.
M&M Federal Savings and Loan
 Association*
McGregor Metalworking Companies*

Martin, Browne, Hull & Harper
Murray-Black Inc.
New Dimensions Group
Nolte Brass Foundry Company*
Ohio Edison*
The Parker Sweeper Company*
(in memory of) Stanley S. Petticrew
Mitchell A. Reedy
Robbins & Myers, Inc.*
Gwenzilla R. Runyan
St. John's Center*
St. Raphael Church*
Kent and Donna Sherry
Mr. and Mrs. Lowell R. Shook
Society Bank, N.A.*
SPECO Division, Kelsey-Hayes Company*
Springfield Area Chamber of Commerce
Springfield City Schools, Ohio
Springfield-Clark County Joint Vocational
 School District
Springfield Newspapers, Inc.*
Springfield Tire & Battery, Inc.*
Taylor, Campbell & Co.
Taylor Manufacturing Co., Inc.*
Warder Libraries of Clark County, Ohio
Wobbe Cleaners Inc.

*Partners in Progress of *Springfield and Clark County: An Illustrated History.* The histories of these companies and organizations appear in Chapter 8, beginning on page 115.

Bibliography

Allbeck, Willard D. *Theology at Wittenberg, 1845-1945.* Springfield, 1946.

_____. *Clark County Boys in Blue.* Springfield: Clark County Historical Society, 1960.

_____. *A Century of Lutherans in Ohio.* Yellow Springs, OH: The Antioch Press, 1966.

_____. *Springfield in the 1870s.* Springfield: Clark County Historical Society, 1977.

Anderson, Sherwood. *Winesburg, Ohio: A Group of Tales of Ohio Small Town Life.* New York: The Modern Library, 1919.

_____. *A Story Teller's Story: The Tale of an American Writer's Journey Through His Own Imaginative World and Through the World of Facts.* New York: B.W. Huebsch, 1924.

_____. *Tar: A Midwest Childhood.* New York: Boni and Liveright, 1926.

_____. *Sherwood Anderson's Memoirs.* New York: Harcourt Brace, 1942.

_____. *Letters of Sherwood Anderson.* Edited by Howard Memford Jones and Walter B. Rideout. Boston: Little, Brown & Co., 1953.

Atwater, Caleb. *A History of the State of Ohio, Natural and Civil.* Cincinnati, 1838.

Austin, W.F. *History of the Manufactories of Springfield, Ohio.* Springfield, 1838.

Barnard, Harry. *Rutherford B. Hayes and His America.* Indianapolis, 1954.

Bauer, Fern I. *The Madonnas of the Trail.* Springfield, 1984.

Beaver, William C. *The Young Men's Literary Club, Springfield, Ohio, Seventieth Anniversary, 1896-1966.* Springfield, 1966.

Beers and Company, W.H. *History of Clark County, Illustrated.* Chicago, 1881.

Bell, P.G. *A Portraiture of the Life of Samuel Sprecher.* Philadelphia, 1907.

Berkhofer, George H. *An Architectural Guide to the Houses of Springfield and Clark County.* Springfield: Clark County Historical Society, 1976.

Bosse, Richard C. "Origins of Lutheran Higher Education in Ohio." An unpublished dissertation. The Ohio State University: Columbus, 1969.

Carson, Herbert N. *The Romance of the Reaper.* New York: Doubleday, Paige & Co., 1908.

Clark, George G. *History of Wittenberg College.* Springfield, 1887.

Clark County Historical Society. Collections.

_____. *Sketches of Springfield in 1856.* Springfield, 1973.

_____. *Yesteryear in Clark County.* 6 vols. Springfield, 1947, 1948, 1949, 1950, 1951, 1952. Reprint. 2 vols. 1978.

Clark Publishing Company, S.J. *Biographical Record of Clark County.* New York, 1902.

Collins, David R. *Archaeology of Clark County.* Springfield: Clark County Historical Society, 1979.

Coyle, William. *The Frankenstein Family in Springfield.* Springfield: Clark County Historical Society, 1967.

Diehl, Michael. *Biography of Ezra Keller: Founder and First President of Wittenberg College.* Springfield, 1859.

Douglas, Lloyd Cassel. *Forgive Us Our Trespasses.* Boston: Houghton Mifflin Co., 1932.

_____. *Green Light.* Boston and New York: Houghton Mifflin Co., 1935.

_____. *Time To Remember.* Boston: Houghton Mifflin Co., 1951.

Ellis, John M., "Historical Sketch of the Association of the Colleges of Ohio." *Transactions of the Twenty-First Annual Meeting of the Association of Ohio Colleges, 1889.* Oberlin, 1890.

Evans, Walter Brigham, Jr. *Cedar Bog: A Plea for Conservation.* Edited by Mary A. Skardon. Clark County Historical Society: Springfield, 1974.

Everts, L.H. *Illustrated Historical Atlas of Clark County.* Philadelphia, 1875.

Farm and Fireside. Springfield, 1881-1896.

Findlay, James. "The SPCTEW and Western Colleges: Religion and Higher Education in Mid-Nineteenth Century

America." *History of Education Quarterly.* (spring, 1977).

Galbreath, Charles B. *History of Ohio.* 5 vols. New York: American Historical Society, 1925.

Gerber, David A. *Black Ohio and the Color Line, 1860-1915.* Urbana, IL: University of Illinois Press, 1976.

Gist, Christopher. *Christopher Gist's Journals.* Ann Arbor, MI: University Microfilms by Argonaut Press, Ltd., 1966.

Harnes, George W. *George W. Harnes' Ohio State Gazetteer and Business Directory for 1859 and 1860.* Cincinnati, 1859.

Harper, Robert S. *Ohio Handbook of the Civil War.* Columbus: Historical Society, 1971.

Haworth, Paul Leland. *The Hayes-Tilden Disputed Presidential Election of 1876.* Cleveland, 1881.

Heckewelder, Reverend John. *History, Manners, and Customs of the Indian Nations Who Once Inhabited Pennsylvania and the Neighboring States.* Philadelphia: Historical Society of Pennsylvania, 1876.

Hooper, Osman Castel. *History of Ohio Journalism: 1793-1933.* Columbus: Spahr and Glenn Co., 1933.

Howe, Henry. *Historical Collections of Ohio, Containing a Collection of the Most Interesting Facts, Traditions, Biographical Sketches, Anecdotes, Etc., Relating to the General and Local History.* Cincinnati, 1847, 1869, 1889, 1891.

Jenkins, Warren. *Ohio Gazetteer and Traveller's Guide Containing a Description of the Several Towns, Townships, and Counties with Their Water Courses, Roads, Improvements, Mineral Productions, Etc., Together with an Appendix or General Register.* Columbus, 1841.

Johannesen, Eric. *Ohio College Architecture Before 1870.* Columbus: Ohio Historical Society, Historic Ohio Building Series, 1969.

Johnson, Edward R. and Mary L. Johnson. *Our Family's Devotion to Wittenberg*. Springfield, 1977.

Joiner, W.A. *Half-Century of Freedom of the Negro in Ohio*. Xenia, OH, 1915.

Kay, Charles S. "Springfield as a City of Homes and Health." *Ohio Magazine*, vol. 3, 1907.

Keifer, J. Warren. *Argument...for the Defense in the Case of the City Council of Springfield Against the Mayor of Said City*. Springfield, 1866.

_____. *Slavery and Four Years of War: A Political History of the United States*. 2 vols. New York, 1900.

_____. "Springfield and Clark County, Ohio, Historically Considered." *Ohio Magazine*. vol. 3, 1907.

Keller, David N. *Cooper Industries, 1833-1983*. Athens, OH: Ohio University Press, 1983.

Keller, Ezra. "The Church in the West." *Lutheran Observer*. vol. 12, nos. 18-32, Jan. 3, 1845-April 4, 1845.

Keller, Thomas A. "A Brief History of the Negro in Springfield, Ohio, from 1855 to 1910." An unpublished monograph.

Kelly, Richard T. *History of James and Catherine Kelly and Their Descendants*. Springfield, 1900.

Kinnison, William, A. *Samuel Shellabarger (1817-1896), Lawyer, Jurist, Legislator*. Springfield: Clark County Historical Society, 1966.

_____. *Building Sullivant's Pyramid: An Administrative History of The Ohio State University, 1870-1907*. Columbus, 1970.

_____. *Wittenberg in Clark County: 1845-1970*. Springfield: Clark County Historical Society, 1970.

_____. "Notes on Six Wittenberg Authors." *Ohioana Quarterly*. vol. 15, no. 4, (winter 1972).

_____. *Wittenberg: A Concise History*. Springfield, 1976.

_____. *An American Seminary: A History of the Hamma School of Theology*. Columbus, 1980.

Kinnison, William A. and Mary A. Skardon. *World War I, Fiftieth Anniversary: 1918-1968*. Springfield: Clark County Historical Society, 1968.

Klopfenstein, Carl G. "The Removal of the Indians from Ohio." From *The Historic Indian in Ohio* by Randall L. Buchman. Columbus Historical Society, 1976.

Knopf, Richard C. *Anthony Wayne: A Name in Arms*. Pittsburgh: University of Pittsburgh Press, 1960.

Lake, D.S. *Atlas of Clark County, Ohio*. Philadelphia: C.O. Titus, 1870.

Lentz, Harold H. *A History of Wittenberg College (1845-1946)*. Columbus, 1946.

The Literary Club: A Review with Literary Activities and Roster of Officers and Members and Bylaws: Organized October 6, 1893. Springfield, 1969.

Ludlow, John. *The Early Settlement of Springfield, Ohio (The Ludlow Papers)*. Springfield: Clark County Historical Society, 1963.

McCormick, Robert W. and Virginia E. McCormick. *A.B. Graham: County Schoolmaster and Extension Pioneer*. Worthington, OH, 1984.

McMillen, T.C. *The Springfield, Ohio, YMCA: 1854-1954*. Springfield: Springfield Tribune Printing Company, 1954.

Mahon, John K. *The War of 1812*. Gainesville: University of Florida Press, 1972.

Meek, Basil. "General Harmer's Expedition." *Ohio Archaeological and Historical Publications*. 1911.

Mellott, Clifford Wayne. "The Legislative Career of Samuel Shellabarger." An unpublished thesis. Columbus: The Ohio State University, 1960.

Miller, Guy G. *New Boston: Clark County's Vanished Town*. Springfield: Clark County Historical Society, 1955.

Miller, Mary McGregor. *The Warder Family: A Short History*. Springfield: Clark County Historical Society, 1957.

Mills, Dorothy Brain. *Friendship Quilt: Background of History*. Springfield: Clark County Historical Society.

Mills, William C. *Archaeological Atlas of Ohio*. Columbus: State Archaeological and Historical Society, 1914.

Moler, J. Douglas. *Maps of Clark County, Ohio*. From surveys by T. Kizer (1855). Cincinnati: Middleton, Strobridge and Company, 1859.

Moran, Sherwood, and Frances Moran. *The Springfield, Ohio, Symphony Orchestra, How It Started and Where It Has Been*. Springfield, 1969.

Ohio Magazine. "Springfield and Clark County, Ohio, Historically Considered." vol. 3 (1907): 349-358.

Ohio Writers Project of WPA in the State of Ohio. *The National Road in Song and Story*. Columbus: Sponsored by the Ohio State Archaeological and Historical Society, 1940.

_____. *Springfield and Clark County, Ohio*. Springfield: Springfield Tribune Printing Company, 1941.

Pershing, Benjamin H. "Fourth Lutheran Church History." *Fiftieth Anniversary, 1897-1947*. Springfield, 1947.

Policemen's Mutual Benefit Association. *History of the Police Department of*

Springfield, Ohio. Springfield, 1909.

Pollard, James E. *History of The Ohio State University: The Story of Its First Seventy-Five Years, 1873-1948*. Columbus: OSU Press, 1952.

Porter, George H. *Ohio Politics During the Civil War Period: Columbia University Study, No. 40*. New York, 1911.

Potter, Martha A. *Ohio's Prehistoric Peoples*. Columbus: Ohio Historical Society, 1968.

Prince, Benjamin F. "Manuscript History of Wittenberg College." Springfield: Wittenberg University Archives.

_____. *A Standard History of Springfield and Clark County*. 2 vols. New York, 1922.

_____, ed. *The Centennial Celebration of Springfield, Ohio, Held August 4th to 10th, 1901*. Springfield: Springfield Publishing Company, 1901.

Prufer, Olaf H. and Raymond S. Baby. *Paleo Indians of Ohio*. Columbus: Ohio Historical Society, 1963.

Prufer, Olaf H. and Douglas H. McKenzie. *Studies in Ohio Archaeology*. Kent, OH: Kent State University Press, 1967.

Quillin, Frank U. *The Color Line in Ohio: A History of Race Prejudice in a Typical Northern State*. Ann Arbor, MI: University of Michigan Historical Studies, 1913.

Randall, Emilius O. and Daniel J. Ryan. *History of Ohio*. New York, 1912.

Reeder, Albert. *Sketches of South Charleston, Ohio*. South Charleston, 1910.

Reid, Whitelaw. *Ohio in the War: Her Statesmen, Her Generals and Soldiers*. Cincinnati: Moore, Wilstach and Co., 1868.

Rinkliff, George L. *The First Evangelical Lutheran Church of Springfield*. Centennial History. Philadelphia, 1941.

Roberds, Calvin E. *150 Years: From Buckets to Diesels, The Springfield Fire Department*. Springfield: Miller Printing Company, 1978.

Rockel, William A., ed. *20th Century History of Springfield and Clark County, and Representative Citizens*. Chicago, 1908.

Roseboom, Eugene H., and Francis P. Weisenburger. *A History of Ohio*. Columbus, 1956.

Rust, Orton C. *History of West Central Ohio*. Indianapolis, 1934.

Shellabarger, Samuel. Papers. Springfield: Clark County Historical Society.

_____. *Tolbecken*. Boston, 1956.

Shouvlin, Dan. *The Shouvlin Family, 1863-1984*. 1984.

Skardon, Mary A. *The Battle of Piqua ...*

Focal Point in Ohio Revolutionary History. Springfield: Clark County Historical Society, 1964.

_____, ed. *The Diary of Captain Samuel Black: War of 1812.* Springfield: Clark County Historical Society, 1962.

_____, ed. *By Horseback to Ohio: Joseph Keifer's Journal.* Springfield: Clark County Historical Society, 1965.

_____, ed. *Soldiers of the Revolution in Clark County, Ohio, Part I.* Springfield: Clark County Historical Society, 1976.

_____, ed. *The Attack on Fort Liberty and the Battle of Piqua.* Springfield: Clark County Historical Society, 1980.

Slaker, Albert. *Revolutionary War Soldiers Buried in Clark County.* Columbus: Archaeological and Historical Society, 1929.

Springfield, City of, Springfield History Committee. *A Century of Springfield Architecture, 1799-1899.* Springfield, 1970.

Springfield Daily News, The.

Springfield Republic, The.

Springfield Sun, The.

Springfield Tri-Weekly Republic, The.

Stephenson, George M. *The Political History of the Public Lands From 1840 to 1862.* Boston, 1917.

Stephenson and Company. *Directory of the City of Springfield.* Springfield, 1852. Facsimile edition by Clark County Historical Society. Springfield, 1969.

Stewart, Eliza. *Memoirs of the Crusade.* Columbus: W.C. Hubbard Publishing Co., 1904.

Taylor, W.A. *Ohio Statesmen and Hundred Year Book: From 1788 to 1892, Inclusive.* Columbus, 1892.

_____. *Ohio Statesmen and Annals of Progress from the Year 1788 to the Year 1900.* Columbus, 1899.

Todd, Edwin S. *Sociological Study of Clark County.* Springfield, 1904.

Tucker, David A., Jr. "Notes on Cholera in Southwestern Ohio." *Ohio Archaeological and Historical Quarterly* 49 (1940): 378-85.

Turner, Edith I. *It Happened in Springfield.* Springfield, 1958.

Veler, Herbert W. "A Life of Ezra Keller, D.D." An unpublished thesis. Chicago Lutheran Theological Seminary, 1951.

Watts, Ralph. *History of the Underground Railroad in Mechanicsburg.* Columbus, 1934.

Weaver, Norman F. "Knights of the KKK in Wisconsin, Indiana, and Ohio." An unpublished dissertation. University of Wisconsin, 1955.

Weisenburger, Francis P. *The Passing of the Frontier.* vol. 3. *The History of the State of Ohio.* Edited by Carl Wittke.

Columbus: Ohio State Archaeological and Historical Society, 1941.

West, J. Martin. *Clark's Shawnee Campaign of 1780.* Springfield: Clark County Historical Society, 1975.

Wharton, Thomas K. "From England to Ohio, 1830-1832: The Journal of Thomas K. Wharton." *Ohio Historical Quarterly.* (Jan., Apr.) 1956.

Whitely, Amos. *The Whitelys in America.* Springfield, 1922.

Wittenberg University Archives. Thomas Library, Wittenberg University. Springfield.

Wittenberg Quarterly, The.

Wittenberg Reveille, The. 1918.

Wittenberg Torch, The. 1914-1984.

Woodward, R.G. *Sketches of Springfield; Containing an Account of the Early Settlement, Together with an Outline of the Progress and Improvements of This City Down to the Present Time by a Citizen.* Springfield: T.A. Wick and Company Publishers, 1852.

The Young Men's Literary Club, Springfield, Ohio, 1896-1978; History, Charter Members, Former Members, Officers from 1896 to 1978, Essayists and Subjects, Roster of Present Members and Officers, Program for 1978-1979, and the Constitution and Bylaws. Springfield, 1978.

Index